THE MONROE DOCTRINE

THE

MONROE DOCTRINE

An ABC Guide to What Great Bosses Do

LORRAINE MONROE

PublicAffairs

NEW YORK

Published in the United States by PublicAffairs™, a member of the Perseus Books Group.

Printed in the United States of America.

TEXT SET IN ADOBE MINION AND ADOBE FORMATA.

Library of Congress Cataloging-in-Publication data
Monroe, Lorraine.
The Monroe doctrine : an ABC guide to what great bosses do / Lorraine Monroe.—1st ed.
p. cm.
ISBN 1–58648–174–6
1. Leadership. 2. Educational leadership. 3. Executive ability. 4. Management. I. Title.
HD57.7.M637 2003
658.4'092—dc21
2003046801

First Edition

10 9 8 7 6 5 4 3 2 1

To My Family

Henry, David, Terry, Max, Sarah, June, Omar

Ruth Cromer Williams,

James Edward Williams,

Hattie Belle Cromer,

and

Edward Lewis Williams,

all of whom I loved,

who loved and formed me,

and who continue to enrich my life in wondrous ways

CONTENTS

xi ■ Introduction

1 ■ **Aa**
Abandon
Accustom
Analyze
Apply
Ask
Assess
Attach
Awaken

17 ■ **Bb**
Balance
Bear
Believe
Break
Build
Burn

31 ■ **Cc**
Calm
Capture
Change
Check
Compete
Construct
Create
Cultivate

49 ■ **Dd**
Dare
Deepen
Demand
Dream
Drop

61 ■ **Ee**
Emanate
Encourage
Escape
Experience

71 ■ **Ff**
Feel
Find
Focus
Free
Fulfill

83 ■ **Gg**
Give

87 ■ **Hh**
Have

91 ▪ **Ii**
Imagine
Indicate
Inspire
Intuit

101 ▪ **Jj**
Joke

105 ▪ **Kk**
Keep
Know

111 ▪ **Ll**
Leave
Linger
Listen
Live
Love

123 ▪ **Mm**
Meditate
Mingle

129 ▪ **Nn**
Name

131 ▪ **Oo**
Observe
Obsess

135 ▪ **Pp**
Participate
Penetrate
Permit
Pilot
Plan
Prepare
Present
Preserve

151 ▪ **Qq**
Quest

155 ▪ **Rr**
Recall
Reduce
Reflect
Release
Rest
Rethink
Retreat

169 ▪ **Ss**
Sacrifice
Sanctify
Select
Shed
Shelter
Simplify
Stretch

183 ■ **Tt**
Take
Think
Transcend

191 ■ **Uu**
Uplift

195 ■ **Vv**
Value

199 ■ **Ww**
Wait
Write

203 ■ **Xx**
X-ray

207 ■ **Yy**
Yield

209 ■ **Zz**
Zigzag

213 ■ Epilogue: Monroe's Twelve Pieces of Parting Advice

215 ■ Postscript

217 ■ Appendix: The Action Plan Worksheet

219 ■ Acknowledgments

Introduction

Anybody who knows me now will not believe me when I say that up until the fourth grade in P.S. 157, I was shy and retiring. But at the beginning of the fourth grade my life's direction changed. I will never know what Mr. James Cooper (a devilishly handsome African-American teacher) saw in me or for that matter what the other teachers saw who recommended me to him. But Mr. Cooper asked me to run for secretary of the student council. I ran and won, and as they say the rest is history. I remained in the student council for the fifth grade and was voted vice president in the sixth grade. I went on to Junior High School 81, joined the school patrol, and graduated from the ninth grade as school leader with the obnoxious title of Head of Heads.

I lived up to that title without being aware of how awfully snotty I had become until a girl who was fed up with my uppity manner came up to me and said, "You think you hot shit don't you?" I thought for a moment and inaudibly replied, "Indeed."

I went to high school, got into the student council, ran for school president, and lost to John Hershey (who wore double-breasted suits) but was elected senior class president and voted the Girl Most Likely to Succeed.

At Hunter College, I was chosen to be president of Omnibus, our Houseplan (a college-grown "sorority"). After graduation from Hunter at the age of twenty-one, I began to teach. In all the years that followed I never thought about or even had the slightest desire to lead a school. I loved teaching, was good at it, and had two young children for whom I wanted to be home when they came home from school. I was glad to do this. I never regretted not moving up into leadership earlier.

However, when Mr. Leonard F. Littwin, my principal and mentor, said to me, "I think you would make a good principal," he planted a seed that fell on what was apparently fertile ground. For the first time in my long years of teaching I began to think of leading a school. I had been observing all along the leadership skills of some administrators and knew that when I was in the fourth grade I was smarter than a lot of them. So I began to take supervision and administration courses and at a rapid rate accumulated the required number of credits to obtain state certification.

While I was doing the above, I was hedging my bets by finishing a master's degree in English literature at Hunter College. The stars were aligning themselves for my future as a leader because in less than two weeks after receiving the certification, a position for an assistant principal miraculously opened up at Stevenson High School in the Bronx and Mr. Littwin selected me to fill the vacancy.

Four years later, in late August, I was asked to take over the leadership of a troubled high school, Taft High School in the Bronx. It was there that I met a remarkable group of teachers and administrators who worked with me to turn the school around. Although the work was hard, it was pure pleasure. It was a joy to cause things to happen by inspiring and supporting staff in their creative madness. Thinking back now on that work and all that we accomplished, I realized there were three important aspects to my leadership:

1. that I loved the adrenaline rush that I got from watching staff, students, and programs grow and develop under my leadership,

2. that I loved being boss in order to use and expand my abilities to dream up the next projects and programs, and

3. that most people like working for a boss who is also competent, collaborative, and a completion compulsive.

After four years of successful work at Taft, I was asked to go to the Central Board of Education to be deputy chancellor in charge of curriculum and instruction for the New York City Public Schools. I took the job because I egotistically thought that I might be able to do for a great many schools what I had done at Stevenson and Taft. While at the Central Board I did some good work, again with the help of a great team—Peter Engel, Jo Ann Asciutto, and Steve Barrientos. However, my time at the Central Board was brief. I was reassigned to Taft, but I took a leave instead and finished my doctorate, something that I had begun while at Taft, once again hedging my bets.

As so often has happened in my life, chance intervened. I was offered an opportunity to teach graduate courses in supervision and administration at the Bank Street College of Education in New York City. I then backed into national consulting at the request of the Edna McConnell Clark Foundation. Later I returned to the principalship, this time at Frederick Douglass Academy, a new and innovative public school in Central Harlem. This work was so successful that it was featured on the news program *60 Minutes* in 1996.

When I retired from the New York City Board of Education for the second time, I was asked to join four successful retired District 4 superintendents at their organization, the Center for Educational Innovation (CEI). I was asked to head a division called the School Leadership Academy. This work involved coaching principals and their leadership action teams in order to improve student achievement, particularly achievement on state tests. The work went well and was quite fulfilling. But in the year 2000 I decided to start my own business, advice I had given to countless women. Once again, to hedge my bets, for an entire year I worked on getting my new organization up and running. In 2001, the Lorraine Monroe Leadership Institute was incorporated, and on July 1, began to train and coach principals.

■

In each of the experiences described above I gained insight into what makes a great leader and a great boss. This book talks about many of these experiences. It is important to say at this juncture that I use the word *boss* to make a distinction between the two. The word *boss* connotes a different aspect of leadership. Both leader and boss inspire, motivate, and get results. However, the liquid, softer sound of the letter "l" in *leader* speaks the difference. Say *leader* and you think collaboration, conciliation, committees. And now say *boss* and hear the explosive forceful sound of the letter "b." You think no nonsense, brook no interference, no more non-productive meetings. Just do it.

The leader and the boss have the same ultimate goal, which is to produce results. They have the same traits, and optimally, they should be in the same person. The differences lie in how things are done, and the speed at which things get done.

Whether the organization is a hospital, a house of worship, a fraternity or sorority, a family, or a business, it will thrive or fail depending on the abilities of the leader. What's required for success is a leader who can do the hard and necessary things needed to make the organization a place where the mission is being worked on every day, in every place, by every person inside the organization, as well as a place where hard work, success, and innovation are recognized, supported, and rewarded.

The lessons in this book are intended to help you practice the craft of leadership and lead any organization successfully. But you can only rise to the level of an *artist* in this work by tapping into your ancestral bones—the heart, courage, and insight that live at a deeper level than mere skill or craft. If you can combine the hard day-to-day craft of leadership with those unique and secret gifts you were born with, you will be able to lead brilliantly and seemingly by instinct. Speaking for myself, a deep belief in a force outside me that guides and assists me is the final element driving me toward artistry.

The ideas in this book come from the lectures that I give to leaders of schools and other organizations all over the world. Generally, I am asked to talk about the characteristics of a good leader, and I can do that with great facility. However, characteristics are adjectives: Good leaders are *smart, prepared, inspirational,* and so on. But great bosses are great because in addition to having these important characteristics, they act, they *do.* In fact, there are certain things that great bosses do every single day. That's what this book is all about, and that's how I hit upon the idea of organizing it through verbs—words of action, words that describe what great bosses do.

In deciding on the format for this book, I went back in memory to my childhood. When I was a kid, I loved to spend time reading the dictionary. I liked the logic of the words being arranged alphabetically, but for me the most fun was flipping the dictionary open to a page and reading the meanings of words that looked interesting or strange and then flipping again through the pages and stopping at a word that fascinated me. I wanted to design a playful page format with capital and small letters just like a children's dictionary, and I hope that readers will browse my ABC book to find verbs and anecdotes that interest them and confirm their own experience as productive bosses and leaders.

The Monroe Doctrine is written for leaders in every arena. Whether your life is devoted to educating kids, growing a business, running a government agency, marketing products, or building a community, you'll find ideas here that will deepen your understanding of how to inspire your people and make your organization run better. You may learn some new things in these pages. More likely—and just as important—you will be reminded of some simple, fundamental truths that are easy to lose sight of in the complex daily life of a leader.

If *The Monroe Doctrine* inspires you to try one or two new ideas that enrich your life and the life of your organization, I will have achieved my goal in writing it. Enjoy the book, and I wish you success in the profound work of leading others.

LORRAINE MONROE

Aa

Abandon

1. To forsake, to desert. 2. To give up completely. 3. To quit.

- Abandon drainers and naysayers in your personal life, and avoid them in your professional life.

- Abandon unrealistic fears. Life is too short to waste in fear.

■

I had taught middle school for ten years when I decided it was time to teach high school. Well-meaning friends said, "Those high school kids are big and bad." But I thought, "They are the same kids I've been teaching for years. They are just bigger and older. I taught and controlled them well in middle school; I can do the same in high school." And I did!

Later, I took a job as one of the deans of discipline in a high school of over 4,000 students. Before I left my old job, my previous supervisor said, "You will be dealing with the underbelly of the school. Soon, you will come crawling back, begging me for a full teaching schedule." I didn't!

What I learned in my dean's office enlarged my sense of compassion and increased my skills for helping distressed people. Every day I dealt with dozens of ordinary children who'd gotten into trouble because of life circumstances over which they had no control. And I learned a lot.

I learned that some of my fellow teachers provoke and antagonize kids.

I learned that many kids who are victims of neglect and of physical, psychological, and sexual abuse can't speak about their pain—and so they act it out instead.

I learned that the same kid who acts obnoxious and profane in order to get attention and respect from his peers can be a pussycat when you get him alone, one-on-one.

I learned that the parents of troubled kids are as troubled, and often more troubled, than their kids.

I became a better teacher, counselor, and parent as a result of working with the "underbelly" of the school. Thank God I knew enough to abandon the fears that my old supervisor had encouraged me to cling to.

■

Q. What fears are depriving you of the rich rewards of a new and exciting career challenge?

A. Name your fears and examine them in the light of their real causes and the real harm they do—and when you're ready, abandon them!

Accustom

1. To familiarize, as by habit or frequent use.

- Accustom yourself to thinking and behaving as a leader.

- Accustom yourself to success, starting with small accomplishments.

- Accustom yourself to spotting leadership abilities in others—and in yourself—and nurturing those abilities.

■

I began to get accustomed to leadership when I was nine years old in the fourth grade. It was then that I ran for secretary of the student council at my father's insistence. When I asked him, "Should I run, Daddy?" He responded, "What's the question? Run!" So I ran and was elected. It was a turning point for me because I'd previously been shy and retiring, but as secretary I had to learn to stand before my peers, read the minutes that I had written, and amend them according to suggestions.

By the end of the sixth grade, inspired by an innovative and devilishly handsome school leader, Mr. James Cooper, I had learned Robert's Rules of Order and had become vice president. I never looked back, and in every school I attended through college I led one or more student organizations.

The habit of leading should begin early. At home and in school, children need to be given opportunities to lead. Getting accustomed to leading early yields both self-confidence and joy in seeing the success or fruition of a project that you spearheaded. Because I was given the opportunity and training to lead, I knew from an early age how leaders can improve the way people think, solve problems, and make things happen. I also knew that leadership training accustoms the future leader to be a cooperative, contributing follower when it is someone else's turn to lead.

■

Q. Does the idea of being a leader intimidate you a little? Why? What exactly about leadership scares you?

A. Whatever intimidates you, don't let it stop you. Grab the next opportunity, and, little by little, you'll get accustomed to leading and prepare yourself for the Next Big Thing in your life. You'll be amazed at the doors that will open for you!

Analyze

1. To examine something critically so as to bring out its essential elements. 2. To examine something carefully and in detail so as to identify causes, key factors, and possible results. 3. To study factors of a problem or situation in detail in order to determine the solution or outcome.

- Analyze everything in your organization. Start the analysis in your head. Then write down the pros and cons of every action and decision you are considering.

- Analyze with your heart, feelings, and intuition—then go ahead.

■

A great boss must be able to analyze the causes of institutional problems or failures. She must also be willing and able to analyze her own behavior as a contributing factor. This requires three things: solitary self-scrutiny, to-the-bone honesty, and lots of ego strength.

Don't assume that your staff or your trusted assistant will tell you what you need to hear. They may be too intimidated—or too kind—to confront you with the truth about yourself.

I've seen an organization begin to die because the boss was unwilling or unable to honestly analyze his own role in causing an exodus of talented staff members (a common organizational problem).

Imagine that you are facing this same problem. If you are a great boss who wants to remain great, you need to analyze yourself. Start by asking and answering crucial questions about your own leadership methods and style.

■

Q. Am I paying my people salaries commensurate with their services to the organization? Am I including people in planning meetings, brainstorming sessions, and other forums in which important decisions get made? Am I underestimating their contributions to the organization? Am I listening to biased or unwise counsel about my people?

A. It's not easy to confront and answer questions like these about yourself. But there's no alternative to this self-analysis. Strive to be honest and ethical in all your dealings with your talented staff—and constantly analyze, question, and challenge yourself accordingly.

Apply

1. To adapt for a special use. 2. To put into action.

- Apply everything you've learned from every job you've had up to your present position.

- Apply everything you've learned about yourself from play and from sports.

- Apply everything you've learned about yourself from every role you've played in your life—as daughter or son, sister or brother, husband or wife, father or mother, friend and neighbor, student and teacher, leader and follower.

■

Whether you recognize it or not, every job you've ever held has taught you something about leading well.

When I worked in Grandpa Ed's fish and produce store, located across the driveway from his house in Potter's Crossing, New Jersey, I learned that every customer expected to be recognized as important. Each one wanted to be served as soon as he or she arrived, no matter what time of day it might be or how preoccupied I might feel.

One man who lived alone way back in the woods would wake me very early in the morning by banging on the side of Grandpa Ed's house. I would get up and cheerily serve him, filleting fish, weighing potatoes and onions, and packing up a cabbage and a box of cornmeal and lard. I had seen my grandfather behave this way, and I learned to do the same. That's how Grandpa Ed kept his customers. More important, that's why they respected him as a merchant and a person.

Later, in one of my first paid jobs, I worked in the lingerie department on the second floor of Macy's on 34th Street in New York City. It was a part-time job, and I was called a Saturday Only (even though I also worked the late night shift on Thursdays). Dealing with the customers wasn't easy.

They'd ask to see *all* the available colors of the slips, then either choose the white one on display or ask for a color we didn't have. If they chose the white one from the counter, they'd ask, "May I have a fresh one from underneath?" I learned to say, "Of course, Miss," with a smile and produce a fresh one.

Whenever I observe how many businesses are run, I am particularly struck and vexed by the absence of the attention paid to service to the customer. I learned early on in my Grandpa Ed's fish and produce store that it was important to serve and satisfy the customers. I apply this lesson to my customer/clients who were my students and I attribute my success to paying attention to service. My advice to bosses who hire or inherit staff who exhibit the following behaviors is to let them go. Let go staff who do careless shabby work. Let go staff who are frequently late or absent. Let go staff who treat customers as intrusions into their private conversations. Let go staff who are subtly insubordinate. Let them go, otherwise they will kill the organization or you. Follow my mentor's advice, which he got from his mentor, "I don't get ulcers; I give ulcers." Remember you are in business to serve customers. If you don't want to serve and satisfy customers, get into another line of work where you don't have to deal with people.

■

Q. What three lessons from former jobs can you apply or adapt to being a great boss today?

A. No matter what business you are in—from education to law to computer sales to fixing washing machines—there are lessons you have learned that you can apply to your present leadership work.

Ask

1. To seek and answer. 2. To inquire.

- Ask "dumb" questions—you may be surprised what the answers teach you.

- Ask for advice from your staff.

- Ask for forgiveness when you are wrong.

- Ask for wisdom to do and say the right things each day.

■

Some bosses think that they are the sole possessors of wisdom. They think that asking others for advice is a sign of weakness, and they feel that they will be diminished in the eyes of their employees if they ask for help. Smart bosses know better. Smart bosses hire smart people, and then they learn from them—for the good of the organization.

When the boss asks his staff members, "What do you think?" or "How would you do this?" or "Got any ideas about how we could solve this problem?" he not only learns new things but also comes off as a leader who respects and appreciates his people. They in turn feel flattered by their boss's attitude, and they are likely to turn their performance level up a notch or two: "My boss *needs* me," they think, "I'd better not let him down!"

■

Q. Who are the two or three people in your organization you feel comfortable and confident about asking for advice?

A. Smart staff members can make the boss look brilliant. Seek them out, ask their advice, and cherish their opinions.

Assess

1. To determine the size, importance, or value of.

- Assess the risks in any really new course of action. Consider how to minimize risks, but don't let them stop you from innovating.

■

At Taft High School, I had a small group of six assistant principals who made up my personal think tank. One was a think-way-out-of-the-tank guy named Michael Mirakian. Shortly after I joined Taft, when I was looking for talented, slightly crazy people to join this group, someone recommended Mike. "You know," she said, "Mike ran our Thanksgiving turkey raffle last year."

"So what?" I responded, "Lots of organizations have turkey raffles."

"Yeah," she replied with a chuckle, "but Mike put the live turkey on display in a cage in the lobby!"

"Wow!" I answered. "That *is* crazy!" I knew that Mike was just the sort of maniac I wanted in my think tank. He's the kind of person to look for when you are assembling your own team of creatively crazy people.

Suppose you had to raise funds for a scholarship, a retreat, an outreach program, a project, or any other worthy cause. Suppose a traveling circus came to town. You need a creatively crazy person to put two and two together and suggest approaching the circus manager about renting an elephant for the afternoon. And then you need a creatively crazy team to expand the idea:

"We can sell the kids elephant rides!"

"And photos alongside the elephant!"

"We can collect elephant dung and sell it to use as garden fertilizer!"

"And you know what?—I know where we can get a camel, too!"

■

Q. Maybe as you read these lines, you're thinking, "What about the insurance risks?" "What if the elephant steps on someone's foot?" "What if the dung contains bacteria?—We could get sued!" "What if . . . ?" Aren't there risks in thinking outside the box?

A. Of course there are. There are risks with every creative new idea. But don't let the risks stop you! Assess the risks, make plans to control them . . . then go ahead, with care and prayer.

ATTACH

1. To bind, fasten, tie, connect. 2. To attribute or ascribe.

- Attach value to what you do each and every day.

- Attach yourself to like-thinking, like-acting people.

- Attach yourself to your function, not to your position or title. That is, ask yourself, "Now that I've received the title of boss (manager, CEO, principal, partner) what is the *function* I must perform?"

- Attach an appropriately balanced value to money, success, prestige, competition, family, relationships, and health.

■

My first job as anybody's boss was being an assistant principal in a huge high school of over 4,000 students. On my first day, a man appeared in the office unannounced, braced himself in the doorway, glanced around, then stared at me and said, "Oh, I see why you wanted to be the boss. You've got a secretary and *two* phones."

I returned his stare and said, "Get out!" He did.

He really thought that the trappings of the office were significant to me. But I knew that the title and the modest perks that went with it were unimportant. My new job really represented a future of hard work and opportunity to do splendid, productive work.

The boss's title doesn't represent a high place on the organizational chart as much as it represents a *function*—a set of tasks that the great boss must *do*.

■

Q. Are you overly attached to your job title and the trappings of power?

A. It's okay to enjoy the perks that come with the title. But you must earn the title and the trappings in the only way possible: by producing results!

Awaken

1. To cease sleep or to come out of a sleeplike state. 2. To rouse, to stir up. 3. To give new life to.

- Awaken in your staff the "why" of the organization, using small meetings, dinners, pep rallies, and chance encounters to infuse people with a sense of purpose and meaning.

- Awaken a renewed vigor in yourself, using solo reflection and self-examination time to explore the following questions:

  What is going on around me?

  Is it positive or negative?

  Am I still getting a charge out of organizing and doing the work?

  Why am I in this business?

  Can I recharge myself personally and professionally so that the others around me will stay pumped?

- Reawaken a sense of the organization's mission in your entire staff at least three times a year.

■

In running schools and other kinds of organizations, I've found it's important to rev everybody up on Day One, then reawaken their spirits and dedication periodically during the year. The organization's momentum slows between Thanksgiving and Christmas, Chanukah, and Kwanzaa and the short dark days of winter. If no outlet is provided for the slump times, teachers and children alike begin to behave in bizarre ways. Parties and charitable works—for example, distributing Thanksgiving baskets to the homeless and caroling for children in hospitals—are helpful ways of shifting the focus away from the rigors of winter and the universally felt, unspoken physical and financial drain of the holidays.

Similarly, when spring comes, everyone gets restless. Many seem to forget what business they are in and why. Great bosses sense this seasonal restlessness and initiate fun activities and projects that keep their staff focused on the work.

■

Q. When was the last time your staff heard the mission from the mouth of the boss?

A. Reiterate the organization's mission the very next time you meet with your staff—and do it again, in a variety of ways, on every possible occasion, in order to reawaken in them their original passion for the organization's goals and ideals.

Bb

BALANCE

1. To weigh by comparing the importance or value of. 2. To bring into a state of equilibrium.

- Balance work with play.

- Balance worry with work.

- Balance diet with exercise.

- Balance hands-on with drop-hands.

- Balance presence with absence.

- Balance carefree with concern.

- Balance grasping with letting go.

■

I am a Libra (October 10); my astrological sign is the scales. Perhaps that is the reason I have always been deeply attuned to the importance of balance in work and life.

Maintaining balance in my personal life is something I work on constantly and rather successfully. The key is controlling my calendar. Because I sometimes get out of balance—obsessing about the Next Big Thing or the latest crisis and throwing myself into the work at the expense of healthy rest and recuperation—I deliberately schedule work *and* play, including both small play (movies and restaurants and outings with friends) and big play (weekends and vacations and sabbaticals).

■

Q. How balanced is your schedule? Does your life regularly include time for work, play, family, and solitude?

A. Take a fresh look at your daybook. If your life is out of balance, make appointments with yourself and with your loved ones so that no aspect of life is neglected.

BEAR

1. To carry, hold, or endure.

- Bear yourself as boss in such a way that you testify by doing what you say and what you believe in. When you do, your staff will then see that you model for the organization what you *expect, inspect,* and *respect.*

- Bear witness to the organization's mission every day by being a:

  Planner

  Producer

  Innovator

  Celebrator

  Reflective practitioner

  Flexible doer

- Bear witness by being:

  Present and punctual

  Intense when necessary

  Kind when appropriate

  Hard-nosed when necessary

  Ready to laugh, unashamed to cry

■

To bear witness as a leader, you must model those behaviors that you ask of your followers. To bear witness means that your actions match the beliefs that you articulate to the public and in private meetings with your staff. I visit many schools and equal opportunity institutions in the course of the year. I am frequently told by the leader or by his assistant what the organization's mission is. But when I walk around, both escorted and alone, I am able immediately to figure out who or what is really important. I see, for instance, who is deemed more equal, more qualified, more cherished, and more gifted and talented. In schools in particular, I can determine who will succeed because of ability tracking and all that tracking means in terms of teacher quality, levels of expectation, and concrete examples of the children's experiences and exposures. I can also determine who will remain gifted and talented and who is clearly deemed and doomed as unteachable and unreachable. What happens to the biblical "least of these" and what happens to the chosen few bears witness to what the leader truly believes and what she truly wants to have happen.

The multitude of poor schools and failing big and small businesses bears witness to the negative beliefs, policies, and personal and personnel practices of the boss. When I said to the staff of my first principalship, "I want you to plan and be magic," they witnessed that I was an indefatigable planner and that I actively encouraged and supported innovation (magic). I bore witness to what I believed because I monitored staff performance and supported innovative ideas. They saw that the results of the plans that we made were astounding. We created an honor class of students, all of whom were accepted to college. We resuscitated both a junior and a senior National Honor Society (Arista). We held assemblies. We reopened the moribund school store. We expanded community service projects. We began fund-raising projects. We created external friends of the school, composed of a group of local business and community movers and shakers who gave the students jobs, internships, scholarships, display space, and good publicity in the neighborhood. In short, words alone will not rally staff for long. It is the boss's bearing witness to her beliefs and steadily working the message that brings results.

■

Q. What are you bearing witness to each day, on the job and in your life?

A. Reread the list above. Examine your life and, if necessary, make some midcourse corrections, so that what you most deeply believe and what your daily life bears witness to are one and the same.

BELIEVE

1. To accept as true or real. 2. To have confidence in.

- Believe in yourself as a leader—that you have the skills, capacities, and strength to lead.

- Believe in what you are about, that your work is worthy, and that it contributes good to other people.

- Believe that no one else could do the work quite the same way— that you are unique. Is this egotistical? No, because it's simply true.

- Believe that you were sent to do *this* work at *this* particular time, and that there is nothing else you would rather be doing now.

- Believe that the plan is working better than you had anticipated. Whether you see it or not . . . it is.

■

When the challenge came for me to assume my first job as a principal, I accepted the responsibility without hesitation. I felt ready for the challenge for two reasons: first, because of the success I'd experienced and the painful and delightful lessons I'd learned in my previous work; second, because I believed what my gut was telling me—that it was time to step up as a leader.

One short year before, the situation had been very different. I'd been asked by my superintendent to accept a principalship twelve months earlier but I did not feel that I was ready. I believed that I was not ready . . . and I was right. I needed another year's seasoning under my mentor, Leonard F. Littwin. After another year on his team I was raring to make the next move.

■

Q. Do you believe you are prepared for your next great challenge?

A. Tune in to what your gut is telling you. When the message is right, believe your gut—and go ahead.

BREAK

1. To separate into or reduce to pieces by sudden force.

- Break rules that don't make sense for the way you work or think.

- Break rules and mandates that stifle creativity.

- Break traditions that are no longer meaningful . . . and create new ones.

- Break the habit of micromanaging, that is, constantly rechecking and making sure. You will never be absolutely, positively, 100-percent sure. So break free and go ahead!

■

A principal whose work I admire once remarked, "If you're not breaking at least one rule a day, you're not doing a good job." This is true in almost any organization, but especially in organizations that are rigid, bureaucratic, and spirit stifling. Only make sure you pick the *right* rule to break—which is an art in itself!

I once got a telephone call from someone in the office of the coordinator of special education. I'll call her Mrs. Gradgrind. "Dr. Monroe," she began, "You have a student named Abdul Jones who was receiving resource room services in his elementary school. I'm calling to check whether he is still receiving this mandated service."

"No, he is not," I replied. "He's doing pretty well in regular classes, and besides, we don't have a resource room here."

"But he must get resource room services," she answered. "It's mandated."

"Abdul has been here for nearly two years," I commented. "What took you so long to ask about him?"

Mrs. Gradgrind ignored this question. "There's an elementary school right next door to your building," she said. "Abdul can go over there and use their resource room."

"Are you kidding?" I shot back. "You want me to send this big eighth grade boy to sit in a room with little kids?"

"You have to—it's *mandated*," she replied, as though the word alone settled the matter. "Dr. Monroe, I'm coming over there right now to see about this."

I hung up the phone and sent for Abdul. I asked him whether he felt comfortable in his regular classes.

"Yes," he replied.

"Fine," I said. "Listen, Abdul, you know all of the teachers and staff members here, don't you?" He nodded. "Well, there's a lady you *don't* know who is on her way here to look for you. When you see her, I want you to disappear. Run the other way, or duck into the boys' bathroom. You can do that, right?"

Abdul agreed enthusiastically, pleased to be part of this new and curious game.

Mrs. Gradgrind turned up at our school—not just that day, but several times. She never could find Abdul. Finally, she confronted me and asked me where he was. "There are 500 students here," I replied. "How can I possibly know the whereabouts of every one?"

Exasperated, she returned to the district office. The next day, Mrs. Gradgrind's supervisor phoned me.

"Dr. Monroe, this is the special ed supervisor. I'm calling about Abdul Jones. You know he's mandated to receive special services . . . ," and she began reciting chapter and verse of the departmental rules that I was violating by permitting Abdul to stay in his regular classes.

I held the phone at arm's length until the sounds from the receiver finally ceased. I let the silence hang in the air for a moment. Then I said to the supervisor, "Let me ask you one thing. If Abdul were *your* son, would you be pursuing this?"

The supervisor made no response. I hung up the phone, and I never heard another word about Abdul from anyone in the district office.

It turned out that Abdul was a very talented youngster. He became deeply involved in theater and dance, both at school and on the outside, and ended up graduating with his regular high school class (just six months late). If I'd followed the rules and forced him to get academic help by sitting in "the baby class" next door, he'd almost certainly have dropped out.

Don't be afraid to break rules for the good of others. Great bosses do!

■

Q. Have you broken any rules lately, for the good of others or for the good of your organization?

A. Break rules that hinder the mission—and have fun doing it!

BUILD

1. To produce as a result of effort. 2. To establish, erect, or enlarge.

- Build confidence and effectiveness in your staff through continual training and monitoring.

- Build on other people's successes by congratulating them, in person or in writing, immediately—the same day.

- Build institutional ways of doing the work that are so right and so solid that when you are absent and after you leave, the institutional ways will endure.

■

Well-built institutional structures stand the test of time because they are deeply imbedded in rightness of purpose rather than in personality.

I was very proud of the things I accomplished during my second stint as principal of the Frederick Douglass Academy. As principal not only did I have to build belief in the radical concept that a college preparatory high school in Central Harlem could and should exist, but I also had to build policies and practices that made the belief happen. My staff and I put the following building blocks in place that produced higher rates of graduation and college acceptance than the school had ever seen. For example, we promulgated a set of Twelve Non-Negotiable Rules and Regulations that had consequences that we enforced. We established a uniform dress code. We built academic rigor into the curriculum by immediately addressing academic weaknesses in reading and math through tutorials both voluntary and mandatory in order to help students pass standardized tests and become competitive for college acceptance. We established ceremonies and rituals that created a predictability to the unfolding year. We formed a yearly calendar of events similar to what great private schools have established over time. We held frequent assemblies for orientation, inspiration, entertainment, celebration, and midcourse correction to remind students of the mission.

We established an entrepreneurial course for all ninth graders and a Whole Life Management Orientation course for all incoming students, which was repeated for eleventh graders to focus on success in college. We expanded the physical education program to include tennis, fencing, Tai Chi, and weight room activities. We offered Japanese, Spanish, French, and Latin and were able to have foreign travel funded so that selected students went to London, Paris, South Africa, Canada, and Israel. We began a Women's Group for mothers in the Academy and even had a school flower and vegetable garden.

No organization, no matter what the business is, can operate without what the above builds: expectations for behavior, expectations for professional dress, preparation to be competitive, institutional ceremonies and rituals, frequent meetings whose agenda vary but whose function is to build institutional commitment and memory.

When the time came for me to move on, I had the fear that all great bosses have—will what I put in place remain? I feared that the policies and practices I'd built concerning college preparation might fall by the wayside.

My main fear proved to be unfounded. The school's graduation and college acceptance rate has remained high. That's a sign of *real* success—built on institutional change rather than personality.

■

Q. Look around your organization. What have you built that stands outside and apart from your own personality, presence, and energy?

A. Build a solid foundation for your organization by finding new ways to do things. Look for opportunities to build new ways of working into the foundations of your organization—into the habits, systems, thought patterns, and assumptions of everyone you work with. Those changes will have a chance to endure and benefit the mission long after you've departed.

BURN

1. To give off light and heat; to contain a fire. 2. To yearn ardently.

- Train yourself to "burn brain" when necessary, that is, develop the ability to focus intensely on a project or plan for three to four hours at a time.

■

Sometimes the mission, the madness of the daily work, and the pressure of due dates demand this ability to burn brain. Burning brain means saying to myself, "Sit down *now*, Lorraine, and don't get up until the whole thing is done." I use this method especially for writing proposals, fleshing out new plans, and developing blueprints for innovations or radical changes. For me, this kind of work is best done not in small increments but all at once, using a concentrated dose of energy.

The burn-brain method requires self-discipline. It also requires preparation. Before I sit down with pen and paper to pour out my plans, I have usually been developing ideas in my free time, during odd moments of idleness at work or while traveling. Thus, the initial raw notes for any new project are often scrawled on dinner napkins, matchbook covers, airplane barf bags, and ATM receipts. But the real work of turning out a working document is produced by the burn-brain method.

■

Q. What is your personal method for getting things done under pressure?

A. Get to know the self-management techniques that succeed for you—no matter how idiosyncratic they may seem to others—and work them ceaselessly.

Cc

CALM

1. To free from agitation or disturbances. 2. To make tranquil, still, and quiet.

- Calm yourself before an unavoidable confrontation by scripting what you want to say.

- Calm yourself before a confrontation with a difficult staff member by remembering that *you* are not on the carpet; he or she is. You are the boss, and everybody on the staff is watching to see who will win. Therefore, remain calm and win!

■

I have had a few confrontational staff members in my schools. They were usually incompetents. I resented them wholeheartedly because they took my time and energy away from doing creative things with their wonderful colleagues.

One such person stands out in my memory—a real T.W. (Time Waster). He gave long written classroom assignments that required nothing of him; for example, "Read all of Chapter 34, entitled 'Major Outcomes of the Crimean War,' and answer all of the questions at the back of the chapter." While the students dutifully did this time-wasting busywork, Mr. T.W. sat quietly at his desk engaged in his own thoughts.

His department chair and I observed him and met with him about his nonexistent teaching—to no avail. After my second observation, I asked, "May I see your plan for the lesson that I just observed?"

T.W. responded, "I don't have it with me."

"Okay, then, let me see the plan from yesterday's class."

He replied, "I threw it away."

"Do you have a plan book?" I persisted.

He said, "I don't have one. I plan on 3 x 5 cards and tear them up when I'm finished."

I thought, "You are indeed finished."

In our follow-up post-observation conference, I reminded him, "Planning is the sine qua non for good teaching." He looked bored. Then he held forth on his teaching and planning philosophy, and I remained very calm as I wrote down what he said: "I left today's plan at home. I ripped up yesterday's plan. I don't need plans because they are in my head. Actually, I don't usually plan because I'm a spontaneous kind of teacher and I don't plan because sometimes the students' immediate interests give me the direction for the day's lesson."

I incorporated these inanities in my written reports to him, which surprised and rattled him. After several such meetings and reports, he said to me, "You know what, Ms. Monroe—from now on in these meetings, I will not respond to you. In fact, I refuse to speak to you at all."

My calm response was, "Could you say that again slowly? I don't want to misquote you in my next report."

Of course, T.W. received an unsatisfactory rating at the end of the school year. He ultimately left our school—but unfortunately not the school system.

■

Q. Is there a person on your staff who shouldn't be?—who drains energy and effectiveness from you and your organization through needless confrontations?

A. Calm persistence and sticking to what's right will enable you to overcome confrontational staff members in any organization. Confront the time wasters in your organization with great calm. After the confrontation calmly write a memo in which you state exactly what happened and what understandings were reached in the meeting. Use expressions like, "On such-and-such a date we discussed this issue or behavior, and we agreed on X . . . therefore, I expect A to happen, and you can expect B to happen." Get this Memo of Understanding to the person you've had to confront as soon as possible. If necessary, have your secretary or assistant witness its delivery.

Capture

1. To gain or win control of. 2. To captivate and hold the interest of. 3. To record in a permanent file.

■ Capture, on a pad kept by your bedside, the great thoughts that occur to you in the middle of the night. Use a night-writing pen or flashlight so that you can decipher your 2:00 A.M. flashes of brilliance.

■

As a new school administrator, I received some of my best insights while trying to sleep . . . or while actually sleeping. I often woke with a start, realizing that a small, insistent voice had been speaking to me, offering an insight, a suggestion, or a solution that demanded to be captured.

Lorraine, the voice might say, *you need to pay more attention to your star teachers. The turkeys are taking up too much of your time.* I'd wake up and be startled by the relevance and wisdom of this insight.

In other cases, I would be tossing and turning in bed, trying to figure out why a promising project I'd launched was sputtering and failing. At three in the morning the source of the trouble would suddenly strike me. *Of course,* I'd say (often out loud), *the problem is that Josh is the wrong person to head the project. Now, who is the right person?* And the name would come to me in a flash—often the name of a person I would never have thought about in the hurly-burly of daily activities.

Why do such wonderful, fresh insights tend to come to us while in bed? Maybe Psalm 16:7 says it best: "I will praise the Lord, who counsels me; even at night my heart instructs me."

■

Q. Are there solutions you seek . . . but can't seem to capture?

A. Let go of the conscious effort to find a solution and let the unconscious work for you. The solutions will come, often when you are busily focusing on other things. Your job is to recognize the solutions when they appear and then to capture them.

CHANGE

1. To alter or modify. 2. To make different.

- Change the direction in which you're looking. In the words of David Bowie, "Turn and face the strange." When you do, the strange becomes the obvious. It was always there for you to see, but you persisted in looking in one direction—the old, habitual, always-did-it-that-way direction.

- Change the way you use your most productive time.

- Change how you feel about change.

■

The hardest change for me when I became a leader was to stop trying to do it all myself. I had to learn to delegate and check some aspects of the work, that is, to trust other staff members' competencies and allegiance to the mission. I think all bosses who are highly successful doers wrestle with this important administrative necessity. As the organizations that I led became larger and more complex, I realized that I had to change from being sole doer and possessor of exactly how the dream should be accomplished to a leader who could choose and release good assistants.

In all of the leadership positions that I've held, I've developed a very good eye for talented individuals to whom I could with very little hesitation and trepidation delegate crucial work. I have been extremely lucky to inherent Artie Sievert, Gerry Bell, Peter Engel, Roberta Goldman, Barbara Armellino, Jo Ann Asciutto, and Steve Barrientos and to choose Dr. Lonnetta Gaines, individuals who helped me to change because they were so in sync with what I wanted to accomplish and with the fast pace at which I work. That was helpful to me so that I could change from thinking that I had to do it all to doing what I love most— monitoring the dream and planning the Next Big Thing. I wish every leader reading this to have remarkable assistants.

The following comical incident happened after I had changed and begun to delegate responsibilities. Late one Thursday afternoon as Mr. Engel, my assistant principal, and I sat working, the coordinator for student activities happened to pass by my open door. I called out to him, "Hey, Mr. Luftkopf, everything set for the junior trip tomorrow?" He stopped midstride, walked slowly to my office door, and looked at me and Engel with eyes that were so pale blue-gray that I swear you could see through the back of his head to I-95. "Everything's fine," he said, "except I couldn't get any buses."

"What!" I yelled, "You don't have any buses for the junior trip tomorrow?" Questions were popping out of my mouth like machine-gun bullets. "So when were you going to tell me?"

"I don't know, I don't know," he stammered.

"Did you call several bus companies?"

"I didn't think . . . "

"Do you realize the entire junior class will be lined up outside the building tomorrow morning and there'll be no buses? What were you thinking? Or did you think at all?"

As he stood opening and closing his mouth with no sounds coming out, I said, "Go home. Go home now."

Fortunately, Engel came to the rescue. He went to his office, called several bus companies, got the buses, and no student or staff member was the wiser except Luftkopf, who was relieved of his position on Monday morning and replaced Monday afternoon with a talented woman. My fault, really. I hadn't checked, but I learned three valuable lessons: delegate and check (if you don't follow up there is foul-up), hire great assistants, and always have talent in the pipeline because as the saying goes, "One monkey don't stop no show."

■

Q. What's the hardest change most leaders have to make?

A. Change—change your organization, change your staff, or (hardest of all) change yourself.

Check

1. To practice being heedful, intent, observant.

■ Check details. As the saying goes, "The third time is the charm, and a fourth time does no harm." It is the little things you *forget* to check that trip you up and derail your grandest plans.

■

All the details necessary to accomplishing a major goal need to be charted, shared, and checked daily if a successful outcome is to be achieved. A great boss follows up (or has an assistant follow up) on every note, every memo, and every directive—even at the risk of having her crack team say, "Okay, okay, we know the drill!" Drill on, because God and success are in the details!

We were nearing completion of one of our routine projects when my associate asked me a simple question: "Have the videotapes been packed?"

These were important to our presentation. The answer was "Yes."

The comeback was, "Has that been checked off the checklist?"

All eyes went to the poster-size checklist we'd dutifully stuck on the wall. Sure enough, not a single item had been checked off.

Things had been done perfunctorily, and since we had done this project so many times before, we felt that there was no need to check things off. Upon checking, we found that indeed the videotapes had been packed, but the equally vital workbooks had *not* been.

So everything we'd packed had to be unpacked and checked off, reinforcing why it's called a checklist. The project went off without a hitch.

■

Q. Who in your organization makes checklists? Who checks them?

A. Every project needs a checklist, and every project must be assigned a detail person with the authority to prepare the checklist and check off the items as they are completed. Otherwise, some detail will fall through the cracks . . . potentially killing the project.

COMPETE

1. To contend or strive for in rivalry, as for a prize.

■ Compete for excellence against other organizations like yours.

■ Compete against your Last Personal Best (LPB). Strive constantly to be better than you were before—individual by individual, level by level, department by department.

■ Compete for a reason, not just for the rush of winning.

■

I learned about LPB from my son's incredibly successful coach, the great developer of young runners, Irv Goldberg. He told his charges, "I don't want you to run faster than the fastest kid on the team; I just want you to run faster than you did the last time." Irv's runners took his advice to heart, and soon they were New York City champions.

Caution: Competition can be detrimental if it's focused on inappropriate goals. I personally am a highly competitive person—I like to win. This fondness for winning for many years spilled over into driving, which I love. I hated to be passed on the highway, especially by a guy who would pull up beside me and give me a sidelong glance or gesture that I would interpret as saying "Wanna race?" The intensity of the competition would double when he noticed, by the position of my hands, that I—a woman!—was driving a *stick shift*. Then he would look really put out, and we'd end up racing for miles. What an adrenaline rush!

I finally stopped engaging in this kind of senseless, death-defying competition when I realized that I didn't have good answers to the following basic questions:

• Why would I risk damaging the car I love so dearly for the sake of a momentary thrill and sense of victory?

- Who the heck is this guy anyway, and why in the grand scheme of things would I risk my plans and dreams in order to impress or humiliate him?

- For someone like me who wants to live to be 100 years old, how does this activity constitute a growth choice? Is it worth risking my life and the lives of others?

■

Q. Examine your own competitive behavior. Do you compete needlessly or for the wrong reasons?

A. There's nothing wrong with being competitive. You can't be a great boss if you are not a competitive person, but unbalanced competition is destructive to both personal and organizational productivity. Make sure you're competing for the right reasons—to reach legitimate goals.

Construct

1. To put together the parts of something. 2. To set in order mentally; to arrange.

- Construct a plan for your personal growth while building the organization.

- At the same time, construct a plan for your life when you leave your job or position (whether voluntarily or not) or retire so that you can seamlessly go on to the Next Good Thing.

- Construct a list of the ten things you've always wanted to do or the ten places in the world you've always wanted to go. Then construct concrete plans to make these dreams real.

■

Both of my parents left their jobs without plans for the future. Both suffered tragic consequences. My father was given the gold watch and dinner at the age of sixty-five (the mandatory retirement age) and went from being a supervisor of men on Friday to having no reason to get up on Monday. There was no one to talk to, no one to boss—in short, nothing to give meaning to his life.

Within months, Dad suffered what everyone thought was a heart attack. But the pain lingered, and it proved to be cancer of the left lung. Sure, he'd always smoked at least two packs a day and had worked in a metal refinery, but my uneducated guess is that—knowing the strength of his will—Dad had unconsciously kept the cancer at bay while he was on the job because he was too involved, too happy in his work to allow the disease to conquer him.

Several operations seemed only to make Dad more and more vulnerable to the spread of the cancer until, one day, he said to me while sitting on his couch smoking a cigarette, "I'm not letting them cut me anymore, Baby." He died soon afterward—within a year of his retirement.

Mama retired at sixty-two because, as she told me, "Raine, I've been working since I was sixteen. I need to rest and stay home."

I asked her, "And do what, Mama?"

She said, "Garden, go to Atlantic City, and visit with my brothers and their families."

Sadly, the result was pretty much the same as with my father. Ma did the things she'd mentioned, but those activities did not provide the social and mental stimulation of work. Some years later, she shadowed into Alzheimer's.

I know that medical experts will say that a sudden shift from total engagement to doing nothing does not cause disease or illness, and I'm sure that's true. But I personally take lessons from both my parents' situations. I have vowed never to stop working at something. In fact, I have a five-year plan written out already for my next work.

■

Q. What dreams are you constructing for your work and your life?

A. Whatever your dreams may be, never stop constructing them and working to make them a reality. I plan to always be constructing the Next Big Thing in my life, so that I'll be fully engaged, up to my very last breath.

CREATE

1. To cause to exist. 2. To produce. 3. To bring something into existence.

- Create something with your hands (if your work is mostly brain work).

- Create something with your brain (if your work is mostly handwork).

- Create with hand, heart, and brain to achieve with excellence.

- Create something that others have said you could never accomplish.

- Create and surprise yourself.

■

My husband, our two kids, and I built a log cabin in the woods in upstate New York. We couldn't afford a contractor, so we ordered a kit by mail and put the thing together ourselves. The work turned out to be both family fun and a far cry from schoolteaching. It took us from late June until Labor Day, when Hank proudly drove the last nail into the last roof shingle and the house was truly complete.

The work was hard. I don't suppose the slaves who built the pyramids of Egypt worked any harder than we did or used more primitive methods. We pulled, dragged, and rolled heavy logs and beams, then hoisted them into position slowly and painfully. We dug trenches, hammered ten-inch spikes, and pushed thick wads of insulating material into place. We developed aches in muscles we never knew we had. But economic necessity made us all stronger and more determined that we would have thought possible.

Halfway through the summer, three of us were felled by accidents:

Hank smashed his fingers with a hammer, our son, David, fell from a second-floor perch, and one of the logs fell on my head. We decided, "The house is telling us that it's time for a break," so we stopped work for a brief camping trip to Cape Cod. When we came back, we were refreshed, and we worked steadily and well to complete the project.

In the process, we surprised both ourselves and the neighbors, who would drive by slowly to watch us amateurs (a man, a woman, a boy of twelve, and a girl of ten) creating a log house. It is still standing.

Later, when I took my first administrative job, I keep one of those ten-inch spikes in my desk as a reminder of the impossible things you can do—when you have to.

■

Q. What are you creating today, for your organization and for your life?

A. If the answer is "Nothing," then you are stagnating. Envision a future and get to work creating it.

CULTIVATE

1. To prepare. 2. To raise or foster the growth of; to cherish. 3. To seek the society of.

- Cultivate your staff and yourself. Foster the professional growth of everyone on your team through courses, reading, travel, and intra- and intervisitations with similar organizations for cross-fertilization of skills and techniques.

- Cultivate leadership abilities in your staff members who show promise, so that they can carry on your legacy of excellence.

- Cultivate outside networks and supporters who can contribute to the progress of your dream.

■

When I went to work at Taft High School, I discovered that there was a part-time position of community liaison held by a teacher named Karen Grayson. Her responsibility was to broker school connections to local businesses and to social, political, and religious organizations that contributed community services, internships, and work sites for our students. They also offered scholarships for our graduates, exhibition space for student projects, and food for students who took part in walk-a-thons and other community activities.

This was a wonderful set of connections that enormously nurtured the Taft community, and we did all we could to expand and strengthen them. Each year in the spring, Ms. Grayson organized a luncheon for the Friends of Taft High School. Our benefactors toured the school, had lunch, received certificates of appreciation, and heard our plans for the next year, to which we hoped they would contribute—and most did. I continued this practice when I founded the Frederick Douglass Academy, under the auspices of Superintendent Dr. Bertrand Brown's resource and development team led by Reverend Linda Tarry.

Q. Are you cultivating connections that can help to drive your organizational and personal goals?

A. Brainstorm with your staff to come up with the names of community, industry, social, religious, and political organizations and people that can help to support your organization and its mission. Charge one or more of your staff members with the task of creating and nurturing relationships with these neighbors, and support those staff efforts in every way you can imagine.

DARE

1. To have the courage to contend against, venture, or try.

- Dare to act! When you know deep down what the right thing is, don't succumb to the paralysis of analysis. As my Grandpa Willie Cromer used to say, "Study long, you study wrong."

- Dare to dream and go ahead!

■

I live in the present and I relish it immensely. But at any time I can tell you without hesitation what my future dreams are.

My mother noticed this about me. When I was eleven years old, she said to me, "Raine, you're always talking about tomorrow, next month, next year. You're wishing your life away. Why can't you just live and enjoy today?"

"I do, Mama," I replied. But I went on thinking about tomorrow.

In a way, my mother's advice was strange, especially coming from her. She didn't talk much about the future, but she survived painful circumstances in her marriage and life by quietly, constantly thinking and planning and saving. I often reflect that if I could plan and save as well as Mama always did, I would be wealthy.

Despite Mama's warnings about too much "wishing," I always wished that, when I grew up, I'd be able to help Mama move from our small four-room apartment on Amsterdam Avenue into a house with a garden for her to putter in. Eventually, I did just that!

At my ninth-grade graduation, I won the leadership award given by an organization called The Danforth Foundation. In addition to a medal, I received a small book entitled *I Dare You!* by William H. Danforth. It presents the Four-Fold Development Program: Stand Tall—Think Tall—Smile Tall—Live Tall. I remember being especially moved by the lines, "You can be bigger than you are," "Are you one of the priceless few?" and "Launch out into the deep."

I still have that book, and whenever I am daring myself to do something new and different, I reread it—and take the dare.

When I was being interviewed by two school board members for the job of heading the Frederick Douglass Academy, one of them asked me to describe my dream for the school. I replied, "I want to create a college prep school in Harlem that mirrors a good private prep school."

The two board members glanced at each other, looking a bit startled. Then one of them turned to me with an amused expression and said, "Well, Dr. Monroe, we'll give you a year's trial to see what you can do." It was clear that she regarded my dream as so much hot air. But I had already years before dreamed of such a school and now I had the chance.

I took their gift of a trial year as a dare. They had no idea how much I love dares—and especially how much I love taking them, and *beating* them.

■

Q. What are you daring?

A. Read widely, dream big—and dare to do.

Deepen

1. To make profound. 2. To extend greatly.

- Deepen your understanding of your staff by watching them carefully with loving and concerned eyes so that you, as a great boss, can attend both to their needs and to your organization's needs.

- Deepen your understanding of yourself through self-reflection, meditation, and journaling.

■

It is important in the smooth running of any operation for the boss to know himself. It is a most difficult task to watch yourself in order to figure out who you are and what turns you on (or off) in different circumstances. But it's essential.

I pride myself on my ability to get along with all kinds of people. But there was a girl who came into my life to deepen my understanding of myself and to help me learn an uncomfortable truth about the limits of my people skills.

It happened when my friend Cathy Tierney and I were the two deans of girls. We had a student named Denise, whom I could not stand, for no apparent reason. This was odd, because I got along fine with all kinds of students, including truants, cutters, fighters, teacher harassers, and gang girls. But Denise was different. Something about her made me a little crazy and tempted me to operate outside of my best self. I hounded her and sought her out, hoping to catch her in some wrongdoing. When I did, I promptly wrote up her transgression on whatever paper was immediately available—napkins, toilet paper, torn-off edges of stationery.

Ultimately Denise did something that warranted her getting suspended from school for a few days. I was overjoyed. I thought "Hah! Gotcha at last!" But like any student, Denise was entitled to a disciplinary hearing. At this hearing, attended by her mother; the guidance counselor; the principal, Mr. Littwin; and me, I was asked to give evidence against Denise. I opened her file folder, and the scraps of paper on which I had noted her misdemeanors fluttered all over the table and floor. As I scrambled to gather them up and organize them so I could make a rational presentation of my case against her, the adults looked away, embarrassed, and Denise smirked across the table at me—reveling, as she always did, in how her presence flustered me.

Mercifully, the conference soon ended. Mr. Littwin said, "Ms. Monroe, can you remain for a minute?"

"Uh-oh," I thought, "he has just seen me at my worst." But he also had witnessed and detected what I did not or could not understand about myself.

When the room was empty, Mr. Littwin said, "Lorraine, what happened? I've never seen you so unprepared and unnerved."

"Mr. Littwin," I began in a rush, "that girl, that Denise she's a menace. She's always . . . and I catch her and she never speaks; she just smirks. I can't stand it, I can't stand her. She . . . "

"Now listen," he interrupted. "You're good, you're damned good. But you can't be good for 100 percent of all the girls you see. Give Denise up. Give her to Cathy. There is no shame in that."

"But, Mr. Littwin . . . " I wanted to insist that I could conquer my aversion to Denise.

"No buts," he said. "Give her over to Cathy."

I acceded to his demand. In the weeks to come, I sat in the office opposite Cathy and Denise while they civilly discussed her behavior. Over time, I noticed that Denise was referred to the office less and less often under Cathy's guidance.

It was hard for me to learn that I could not be everything to everyone. Years later I reached a deeper understanding of why Denise was such a nemesis to me. I realized that Denise personified something hidden deep in my subconscious that I did not want to surface, and my hounding of her was an effort to suppress it—whatever it was. Whether this was pseudopsychology on my part or the true explanation of my behavior, the incident with Denise helped me to stop myself whenever I became unreasonably opposed to a person, an idea, or a situation.

Thank you, Denise.

■

Q. How well do you know yourself? How fully do you understand the real reasons behind your emotions and your actions?

A. Difficult as it may be, you must deepen your knowledge of the motives behind your decisions and behaviors. In this way, your decisions can become purer and more completely focused on the forward movement of your organization.

DEMAND

1. To ask for or call for with authority. 2. To require.

- Demand excellence from yourself and others.

- Demand does not (always) mean *command.*

■

Great bosses understand that demanding alone does not produce results. I have found that very often a staff will bitch and moan, do nothing, or sabotage a new demand because they are not adequately prepared or trained to do the new project well or have not been educated enough by the boss to see the necessity or urgency of doing what the boss requires.

To have her demands met, the great boss must do the following:

- Give the rationale for the demand.

- Give clear instructions about how to meet the demand.

- Model what she expects and respects.

- Give training as necessary.

- Give support and encouragement.

- Monitor progress.

- Make corrections as necessary.

- Celebrate success.

- Give new demands.

- Give the rationale for the demand . . . and the cycle continues.

Organizations that work this way produce great things. They consistently beat out the competition and exceed their last personal best.

■

Q. How well do you prepare your staff for the demands created by new ideas and new projects?

A. The most important part of *prepare* is *pre-,* which means "before." *Before* the demand becomes real, lay the groundwork, so that your staff members will receive the new demand as part of the natural, continuing movement toward excellence.

DREAM

1. To see a series of images, ideas, emotions, and sensations occurring during sleep. 2. To daydream. 3. To have a wild fancy or hope.

- Dream of your greatest conceivable achievement.

- Dream your response to those who think you can't achieve.

- Dream a mantra ("I can do this. I can do this").

■

I say to myself—sometimes out loud—"I can do this—I can do this," and I write out how I will do it. And then I do it. Ha!

For more than fifteen years, I had the dream of running my own company and being my own boss (at least, as far as *anyone* is truly her own boss). In the spring of 2001, that dream became a reality. I launched the Lorraine Monroe Leadership Institute (LMLI).

It's funny how powerful and persistent dreams can be. I'd been working successfully under the auspices of another company, but as the years passed, I began hearing an inner voice, repeating the words my mother always used when I was slow about doing something: *Hurry up, Raine. We don't have all day, you know!*

Now I found my mind turning back again and again to my dream of running my own company, and I heard myself saying, *Hurry up, Raine. You don't have all life, you know! Maybe you're planning to live to be 100. But if you're ever going to get started, you'd better get started!*

So I followed my usual practice: I moved the dream to paper. I wrote out step by step what it would take for me to operate independently and to achieve economic self-sufficiency, especially during the first year or two that LMLI would be in business. With this plan in hand, I was ready to take the plunge—and I did.

I had no illusions about the difficulty of starting a new enterprise and making it successful, but I had overcome long odds before. Most important, I had faith in the worthiness of the work and in the abilities that my associates and I bring to the dream. With hard work, prayer, and God's help, dreams do become reality.

■

Q. What's your next dream? What are you doing now to prepare for it?

A. Whether you do something or do nothing, time passes anyway. So dream your dream. Design it! Do it!

Drop

1. To let go, to let fall, to give up. 2. To cease. 3. To release.

- Drop reacting to every moan and complaint you hear.

- Drop dead weight in your organization.

■

If you notice, the chief troublemakers in your organization are the disgruntled incompetents—the members of what I learned to call the NBC Club (the Naggers, Bitchers, and Complainers Club). They delight in detracting and degrading, denigrating and denying—draining the leader and the dream. They come to work every day with that agenda. I think they must suck lemons in their cars on their way to work so they are ready to sour every idea and joyful occasion.

Much of the time, you need to ignore their griping. However, sometimes it pays to listen to and examine what is being said, in case there is some truth to their grumbles. (Sometimes, the complaints of the NBC Club reflect feelings that other staff members share but are too timid or respectful to state openly.) In this case, address the truth quickly and quietly without too much fanfare. Simply state in the next staff meeting or bulletin, "I have noticed . . . and the problem has been addressed."

Of course, it's best to have noticed or anticipated difficulties or glitches *before* the major NBC Club members do. Notice and anticipate results by dropping everything else on your schedule and walking around the organization daily, observing, listening, and interacting. The more often you do this, the less often the NBC Club can surprise you with a justified complaint.

■

Q. Can you name the members of the NBC Club in your organization?

A. Identify the NBC Club members and drop them from serious involvement in the working of your organization's dream. Then turn your attention to galvanizing the doers, who are the majority of your staff members. Remind them of the dream and give them the go-ahead to use their talents and ideas to make the dream happen. Do this openly, in the faces of the NBC Club members—and watch the numbers of Naggers, Bitchers, and Complainers begin to drop.

Ee

Emanate

1. To issue forth from a source, as fragrance emanates from a flower.
2. To flow from.

- **Emanate a positive energy that motivates, captures, and galvanizes your staff.**

■

Emanate is an interesting and perhaps surprising verb to use in describing the actions of a great boss, but I believe something should flow from the leader.

In my lectures on leadership, I refer to the "Intentionality Factor." It is what the leader unconsciously exudes that commands respect, attention, and followership. It cannot be taught or faked, but it can evolve over time, growing from the leader's complete devotion to a mission that totally engrosses him.

In the sixties, to emanate meant to send out good vibrations. A really great boss who operates from selfless motives receives a level of attention, work, and high productivity born out of respect for the boss and what she stands for and believes. Many years after I had gained some skills as a teacher, I came to realize that there was something ineffable that children and some adults felt coming from my intentionality and my deep belief that quality education was life changing, such that my mere standing up and looking around could cause children and adults to come to quiet. This ability amazes me. This happened numerous times: with a class of thirty-six rambunctious seventh graders, in a full high school auditorium, and in the San Antonio coliseum when I spoke before an audience of more than 7,000 educators. I realized that children and adults on all those occasions had given me permission to "control them." I am not sure what it is that I emanated, but I thank God for it.

In the best cases, the organization's mission is pure and about doing good. In such cases, the great boss emanates good intentions from her inner being. Staff members recognize this and acknowledge it by their own unspoken commitment to the organization and by their efforts toward achieving the mission.

If you emanate your own convictions and act with the purest of motives, the people around you will respond with magnificent results beyond your written plans—and your wildest imaginings.

I hold in memory teachers who emanated seriousness, and I hold in memory my beloved relatives, my maternal grandmother, Hattie Belle Cromer, and my paternal grandfather, Edward Lewis Williams, and my minister, Reverend James H. Robinson, all of whom by their way of being and acting even in the smallest particulars of life emanated a dead-on sense of purpose that influenced me to do good things.

Emanate is a verb that is difficult to discuss, but you recognize it when an individual or a boss evidences a high seriousness of purpose and intentionality that says, "This work that we're doing transcends me and you; it is about something larger than all of us put together."

■

Q. What am I emanating as a boss?

A. Let your best-developed self shine through in every act and word.

ENCOURAGE

1. To inspire with courage, spirit, or hope. 2. To spur on, to stimulate.

- Encourage new stars by giving them training to gain competencies.

- Encourage old stars by giving them opportunities to develop untapped capabilities.

- Encourage productive stars by giving them leadership roles.

■

Hire promising newcomers who believe in you and in the mission of your organization. Welcome, develop, and encourage them as they bring new energy, ideas, and optimism to the organization.

In turning schools around, I made it my business to hire new bright people who had little or no teaching experience. As a result, I did not have to teach them how to undo bad habits.

I once hired a young woman, a graduate of Fisk University. She came for the interview wearing a navy blue suit, a white blouse, and sensible pumps—an immediate plus in my eyes. The second plus was that she expressed lively interest in what we were attempting—namely, to create a college preparatory school in Harlem that would emulate the positive aspects of excellent private schools.

Once I'd hired her, whatever suggestion I made, she immediately implemented. What a gift she became for the children and the school! She thrived as a teacher who got great academic results and finally became the coordinator of several of our academic and extracurricular programs.

I encouraged her to think about becoming a school administrator, just as Mr. Littwin had encouraged me. I recently learned that she will soon become a leader of a school that aims to replicate the great things we accomplished at the Frederick Douglass Academy. The boss's encouragement feeds and ultimately multiplies the good that she sees in her employees.

■

Q. Are you developing newcomers and encouraging talented experienced staff for the benefit of your organization?

A. Make it part of your mission to help develop the next generation of great bosses.

ESCAPE

1. To get free of, to break away from. 2. To avoid a threatening evil.

■ Escape the "comfort boxes" in your organization—that is, the boxes of traditions, habits, and contentment that stifle organizational change. List the boxes, then figure out at least three ways to break out of them. (This is a good meeting agenda or workshop item.) Some samples of comfort boxes to get you started:

It's too late . . . it's too soon.

Let's study this more.

We always . . . we never . . .

It can't be done here.

We tried that before.

You're new here.

Not with this staff . . . these clients . . . this community.

Let's form a committee.

■

Comfort boxes are a little like coffins. They confine the boss and cushion her from challenges and tough decisions. It's quiet in those boxes. They offer little room for maneuvering. And they provide a surprising amount of security, respect, and even happiness. After all, at a funeral, the person in the box is the main attraction, treated with dignity and appreciation by everyone who attends. Frankly, some of the people at the funeral are happy to see old so-and-so safely tucked away in her box . . . just as some people on your staff are happy whenever you are safely ensconced in your office, where you cannot make unsettling or uncomfortable demands on their time, energy, or creativity.

Unfortunately, all comfort boxes come with one big disadvantage:

In the end, they're only suitable for burials. The boss who insists on staying inside her comfort box will ultimately get buried . . . as will the organization she runs.

Now a confession: On some Monday mornings, those comfort boxes look pretty good, even to me. But the great boss breaks out of the box, charges ahead of the group, and yells back over her shoulder, "Keep up with me, gang, 'cause I can see forever out there—and it looks terrific!"

■

Q. Which "comfort boxes" are familiar to you from your own organization? Which ones are most important for you to break open in order to move forward?

A. The great boss realizes that an organization that won't break out of its comfort boxes is doomed to be buried or taken over by the competition. Model the right behavior by developing and supporting a handful of pilot projects staffed by the creatively crazy maniacs in your organization.

EXPERIENCE

1. To undergo. 2. To live through events. 3. To observe facts and events in context with what is implied by thought.

- Experience everything (well, almost everything). Great bosses do not limit their experience to just knowing about or loving their particular business. Great bosses lead by having the experiences that invent and recreate themselves and their institutions.

- Experience expansion of chances and choices. Meditate, mow the lawn, watch the sun rise and set . . .

- Experience a variety of things in order to maintain your creative edge. Don't kvetch—stretch!

- Experience by periodically stepping outside of your ordinary activities and:

climb	sing
cook	sculpt
garden	take photos
run	meander
write	fast
hike	spend the weekend in your pj's
swim	drive fast—or slow
dance	take a trip with no itinerary
volunteer	take a different route to work
travel	take the bus to the end of the line
paint	do nothing at all

■

For me, reading inspirational texts or stories, walking alone on the

beach or in the country, meditating and semi-fasting on weekends—
all these help me to stay focused on the mission of my work and life.

A Sunday afternoon spent in a museum is an experience I seek out
frequently. Visiting the Whitney or Museum of Modern Art or the
Studio Museum in Harlem allows me to feed my brain with ideas and
impressions that inform my work. Ideas such as these come to me as I
walk through the galleries:

- Human experience has universal qualities.

- Everything is art.

- Every human being is a work of art.

- The juxtaposition of seemingly unrelated objects redefines how
  I perceive and understand life and ordinary events.

I leave museums head-filled and soul-filled with as much belief and
hope for the world and mankind as I feel when I leave church after en-
joying a great choir or hearing a fine sermon.

■

Q. What new experiences have you had lately? How can these experiences help to make you a better boss?

A. The more varied your experiences, the better dreamer, thinker, planner, doer, and problem solver you will become.

FEEL

1. To be aware of by instinct or inference. 2. To be conscious of an inward impression.

- Feel uncomfortable when days pass and you don't sense progress in the work.

- Feel uncomfortable when any major aspect of the work seems to be stagnant.

- Feel uncomfortable when you notice changes for the worse—especially changes in the behavior or attitudes of your closest assistants.

■

The great boss develops institutional antennae—sensitive instruments of perception that make her feel uncomfortable when something is amiss in the organization. The great boss is so finely attuned to the organization that she can sense the difference in what I call the Organizational Hum—the ever-present vibration of activity, energy, communication, hope, and striving that has a unique pitch and frequency in every organization. Learn to listen for this sound and to diagnose what it is saying about the health of your organization.

When I was a principal, I could feel when things in my school were right or wrong by sensing the quality of laughter, talk, and movement in the halls, in the cafeteria, in the classrooms. Whenever I felt the Organizational Hum getting negative—a little too loud, too harsh, too noisy, too cacophonous, too frenzied—I knew it was time to ask questions and begin probing for the source of the discomfort.

■

Q. Can you sense or feel what is going on in your organization, beyond what your staff tell you and what they put into their written reports?

A. The great boss goes everywhere in the organization and watches the people work. In this way, she feels progress (or lack of progress), job satisfaction (or poor morale), dedication to the mission (or apathy), clarity of purpose (or confusion) . . . and is ready to congratulate, correct, and anticipate the Next New Thing.

FIND

1. To discover through observation, experience, or study.

■ Find time to be really attentive to your children, spouse, and other loved ones. The amount of time you spend with them is not as important as giving them your *full* attention. Hard, I know, when you are obsessing about organizational growth and excellence!

■ Find time to talk to and thank the people in your organization whom you rarely work with—the custodians, the security guards, the cooks in the cafeteria, the man who fixes the elevator. They know a lot, and they make your organization run smoothly every day in ways you've never stopped to think about and that you often take for granted until they are absent and something doesn't work.

■ Find time to do nothing each day, even if it is for only three minutes.

■

My husband and I instituted on-call five-minute talk sessions with our kids following the good-night story and kiss. These little spontaneous chats at the close of the day proved to be wonderful bonding experiences.

Later, when my husband took a job teaching college two evenings a week, he couldn't be home for those talks. As a substitute, the children started compiling "Tuesday/Thursday Books" in which they left notes and drawings for Dad. We still have these precious books and relish leafing through them from time to time.

Every Christmas Day, fifteen to twenty friends and relatives would come to our house for breakfast and stay through brunch and dinner. For many years, my husband and I would follow this hectic, joyous time with two days off at the Plaza Hotel to find and rediscover each other again at the year's close.

■

Q. Whom do you need to find time with to make your life more joyous and complete?

A. Don't make excuses—find the time today!

Focus

1. To center attention on.

- Focus on the mission.

- Focus on outcomes.

- Focus on the positive members of your staff.

- Focus on your health, your family, and your plans for yourself outside the organization.

- Focus on staying fixed on the target. Doing so keeps you centered and sane for your work and your life.

■

I recently gave a keynote address at a educators' conference. During the question-and-answer session, a man asked me, "Should teachers be held accountable for results or evaluated on outcomes?"

I can't imagine a question like this being asked in any field other than education. *Of course* the focus must be on results. And *of course* the outcome to be sought in any educational endeavor, from Head Start through graduate school, must be the same: increased knowledge.

Knowledge takes different forms at different times. In primary school, the focus should be on learning to read and developing a love for reading, directed toward the intellectual and economic freedom that the love of reading brings. In high school and college, there are specific bodies of information that must be mastered—the laws of physics, the facts of American history, the rules of grammar. But in every case, no matter what the business is, the focus should be clear.

■

Q. What are you focused on? Is your staff focused on the same thing?

A. When you lose sight of your focus, the staff does too—and the mission suffers.

FREE

1. To relieve or rid of what restrains, confines, restricts, or embarrasses.

■ Free your staff from the burden of micromanaging. Micromanaging kills spirit and initiative. It will drive excellent staff members to other organizations where they will feel more appreciated.

■

I used to work in a school where I was coaching a very talented and effective principal. He was suffering from daily attempts by someone sent from the Central Board of Education allegedly to "help" him. In reality, the assistance undermined the principal's authority through micromanaging. He was buried under an utterly useless flood of paper, all in the name of bureaucratic necessity.

I've been on the receiving end of the same problem myself. One time, I was asked to become a part-time assistant to the coordinator of an important high school program—an intelligent dynamo of a woman whom I'll call Sandra. I was new to the school and I didn't think she even knew I existed, so when she chose me I was delighted and quite eager to get started and justify her faith in me.

The first time Sandra gave me a task, I began to work on it diligently. Soon, however, I had to go off to teach a class. When I returned an hour or two later, the work was already done. I thought, "Sandra must have needed it more quickly than I thought." But over the next two weeks, I never got to complete even one of the tasks she assigned me. When I asked, "Where's the work I left there?" Sandra would reply, "I did it myself," or "I stayed late last night and finished it," or "I took it home over the weekend and it's done."

After three weeks of this, I realized that Sandra was not only incapable of delegating responsibility but also totally unaware of this incapacity. So I told her, "I want to go back to full-time teaching." She acquiesced without even asking why.

Sandra never realized that she suffered from the same major fault as many other brilliant administrators—the inability to use competent people well, i.e., to free competent people to perform the assigned task according to their talents. Consequently, she diminished her ability to lead by focusing on tasks that others could do.

Sandra never rose beyond the level of the position she held when I worked for her. She retired an embittered woman, feeling she had been unjustly passed over for promotion; she never understood why she was never promoted.

■

Q. Do you micromanage your people? Worst of all, do you micromanage the *wrong* people?

A. Trust your excellent staff members. Micromanage only those who need the guidance to improve their skills.

FULFILL

1. To measure up to. 2. To bring into actuality; to effect. 3. To realize or manifest completely.

■ Fulfill the promises you made when you became the boss.

■ Fulfill the needs of your staff, especially those delivering the goods.

■

The most important promises a great boss makes are those she makes to herself. I have always promised myself that I will work hard and play hard. I schedule some small pleasure in my calendar every week. But the greatest promise I make to myself is this one: "I will leave when the work is not fun anymore." For me, the fun always comes when I can add a new project or introduce a new way of doing the work. When this is impossible, I dull out—and I utterly refuse to dull out either in my personal and professional life.

In one of my positions as boss, I succeeded a supervisor whose behavior impeded the work of her assistants. She'd insisted on reading their every memo and directive and second-guessing most of their proposed actions. Therefore, very little got done in the organization.

When I came on board, I generally skimmed their suggestions and gave the go-ahead. In effect, I was saying, "Look, do your jobs. Do what you think is right on behalf of the students and the school. I will trust you not to mess up." They breathed a collective sigh of relief and began to do remarkable work.

■

Q. Think back to the ways you've been bossed. What promises did you make to yourself about the ways you'd act and be once you became a boss yourself? Are you fulfilling those promises?

A. Don't replicate the horrors of your worst bosses. Instead, release the professionals on your staff to fulfill their ambitions and goals by using their talents and ideas for the good of the organization.

GIVE

1. To place in the hands of. 2. To permit. 3. To accord, to entrust.

- Give people enough time to do their work well—but not too much time.

- Give of yourself as a listener, a shoulder, and a hand. Give of yourself—but always move the mission.

- Give blame appropriately—never to the group as a whole but to the person(s) who messed up.

- Give generous praise to those who've earned it.

- Give people the authority, power, and support to work their dreams in order to make the organization and its people bloom.

- Give up total power, authority, or dream—*never!*

■

Great bosses often find themselves playing the role of social workers or counselors for their staff members, who might see the boss as Mama or Poppa. This perception of the boss by the staff has little or nothing to do with what the boss has said or done but rather with who the boss is as a human being and how staff members experience the boss's humanity.

I remember one post-observation conference where I discussed a teacher's professional work with her objectively for half an hour. The conference over, she rose to leave, then paused at the office door and said, "I just want to say that if you pass my classroom and see me staring out the window and not teaching, don't be upset. It's just that my husband stole my three children yesterday, and I don't know where he took them."

I had to respond both as a mother and as a leader.

"Come back in here and sit down," I said. She did. After a long pause, I spoke. "You have my sympathy. As a mother, I know how heartsick and upset you must be. If you need to stay home, I will understand. And of course I'll do anything I can, personally or professionally, to help you through this time." Through her tears, she smiled at me.

Now came the hard part. "But, you know," I added, "you made the decision to come to work today. So if you step into the classroom, you *must* teach. The children can't pay the price for what your husband has done. Do you understand what I'm saying and why I'm saying it?"

She nodded.

"For what it's worth," I added, "I would come to school and teach if I were you. Work can be therapeutic when you're working through a difficulty. And if you need to talk, I'm here."

■

Q. Are you "understanding" when some of your staff members have trouble producing on the job when their failure harms the organization and impedes the mission? What do you do to help such staff to get back on track?

A. A great boss is compassionate, and understanding, and giving. But the work and the dream of the organization must continue.

HAVE

1. To possess 2. To own, to hold. 3. To acquire.

- Have a good laugh at least once a day.

- Have the ability or develop the ability to appreciate and laugh at the ludicrous or the absurdly incongruous in some events and in some staff behavior.

■

In order to remain sane in this work as boss, you have to have a sense of humor. Without it you lose perspective. There are situations and people that are so extreme that if you didn't laugh, you'd hurt somebody or lose your job.

Early in my teens I reverberated to this quote from Rafael Sabatini's book *Scaramouche:* "He was born with a sense of humor and a sense that the world was mad." Indeed, as a leader I saw and heard things that made me believe for a brief moment that the world had gone mad. However, I found that if I could find the humor in a situation and laugh I could go on.

I still laugh when I remember an incident in which one of my staff who was a Monday/Friday absentee person called and asked to speak to me. In a raspy voice he said the following, "Hello, Dr. Monroe (cough, cough, sneeze). I'm feeling lousy. This cold that I've been fighting all week has a grip on me so I won't be in for a few days (sneeze, sneeze, cough)."

I was just about to commiserate with him when I heard the following in the background, "Last call for passengers for Flight 86 to San Juan at Gate 22. Now boarding all rows . . . " I hung up before he could finish his lie, which started, "Excuse me for a second. Honey—turn down that Travel Channel!"

■

Q. Can you laugh at others and yourself?

A. A sense of humor and a sense of humility will allow you to remain sane, keep perspective, and stay focused on what is important.

IMAGINE

1. To form a mental picture; to envision within oneself.

- Imagine the ultimate success of the organization under your leadership.

- Imagine what that success will look and feel like and write it down. What is doable now? Plan how to accomplish one of the things you wrote down; then act.

■

I have never undertaken any project (including this book) without first imagining on paper what it would ultimately look like.

In every leadership role that I assumed after becoming a teacher, I imagined—that is, I wrote out the vision on paper, the look and accomplishments of the organization Year One, Year Two, and Year Three. It was clear to me that if I did not have a mental picture of what I wanted the program or organization to be like, I absolutely could not articulate the vision to staff or to people outside of the organization from whom I would ultimately seek funding and other support.

To simply imagine without writing out my thoughts is unthinkable to me and utterly impractical, since all the doers who would be responsible for carrying out my imaginings have to be informed and let in on the dream.

Workers who have to guess at the boss's vision or intentions are left to their own imagination and devices as to what they are to do to assist in the fruition of the dream. This can spell organizational disaster.

■

Q. Can you describe, in words or images, your vision of your organization as it will be two years from today?

A. There can be no results without concrete, written imagining . . . and results are the goal of any great boss. Use the newspaper writer's five W's plus H—Who, What, When, Where, Why, and How—or use the Action Plan Worksheet format in the appendix of this book to plan the dream of your organization.

INDICATE

1. To point out; to state briefly; to show.

- Indicate to individual staff members when you are pleased or displeased with them. Follow up with an informal note (keep a copy), and write on your calendar the date of the conversation.

- Indicate in your note exactly what you said to the staff person—the brief specific suggestions you made for change and improvement or what you were pleased to see. These notes are important as reminders to you and to your staff member as to what behaviors you'd like to see more of—or less of—in the future.

- Balance good and bad in the notes you write, so that the organizational grapevine doesn't brand you as a boss who sees only the mistakes the staff makes, and never the good things they do.

■

Clearly indicating your reactions to what you see as you walk around the organization will encourage your staff's growth and development.

I recently visited the classroom of a teacher—I'll call her Ms. Winthrop—who prided herself on being a terrific educator. She was indeed a very smart and caring person. But when I observed her teach, I couldn't figure out the aim of the lesson, either from what I read on the blackboard or from the children's work in their notebooks.

I shared this observation with her principal, saying, "If I didn't understand what was going on, I'm sure the kids didn't." The principal simply nodded and jotted a note to himself.

The next time I visited the school, Ms. Winthrop spotted me in the hall. "Dr. Monroe!" she called out, "Please be sure to visit me before you leave—promise!"

"Okay, I promise," I said, and before I left the building I dropped in on Ms. Winthrop's class.

She was teaching a math lesson, and the blackboard was filled with notes. She had written a warm-up activity, a specific aim with lesson steps, several examples for the students to look at if they got lost, and a homework assignment that reviewed the aim. The purpose of the lesson was crystal clear.

I smiled and gave Ms. Winthrop a thumbs-up. She came over to me and whispered, "I heard you were disappointed the last time you visited me. That wasn't me. You caught me on a bad day." She went on to explain a personal problem she'd been wrestling with.

Later I asked the principal, "What did you say to Ms. Winthrop?"

He said, "Oh, I just told her you weren't pleased with what you saw in her classroom. You see, she respects you so much that she was determined to prove what she could do."

■

Q. Do you indicate orally and in writing exactly what you expect from your staff?

A. When the boss indicates what she expects, the staff will usually respond . . . especially if the boss models what she expects and respects.

Inspire

1. To influence, move, or guide. 2. To exert an animating, enlivening, or exalting influence on.

■ Inspire your staff with the meaning of the mission.

■

TWENTY-TWO INSPIRATIONAL WORDS AND PHRASES TO USE WHEN INSPIRING STAFF

1. Together We
2. Service
3. Purpose/Mission/Calling
4. Challenge
5. The Competition/Us vs. Them
6. Transformation
7. Surpass/Transcend
8. Confirm
9. Engagement
10. Preparation
11. Hard Work/Difficult Tasks
12. Heart
13. Spirit/Will
14. Capacity
15. Collaboration
16. Future
17. Today
18. Plan
19. Dream
20. Faith
21. Persevere
22. Results

I never give a talk to staff, especially at the beginning of a new undertaking, without including the following:

1. A reminder of our purpose.
2. A list of our past accomplishments.
3. An enunciation of our challenges.
4. A description of the competition.
5. A list of our capacities.
6. An outline of the plan.
7. A statement of my faith in our communal effectiveness.

Each of the seven could be paired with another word or phrase from the list, for example, *purpose* could be paired with *dream*, or *capacity* with *hard work*, and *together we* with *collaboration*.

Look at the list and mix or match according to your need.

∎

Q. In what two or three specific ways do you behave as inspirer, guide, and motivator in your organization?

A. Use the inspirational words listed above when it's time to uplift your staff with the energy and strength needed to climb the next mountain or overcome the next obstacle.

INTUIT

1. To attain direct knowledge without evident rational thought. 2. To have quick and ready insight.

- Intuit realities that you can't master through logic.

- Act intuitively. Follow your educated gut—it will often speak loudly and truly to you when you are open and receptive to hearing and heeding it.

■

Everyone knows the expressions "I had a feeling," "Something told me . . . ," "All of a sudden, I felt," "I don't know why or how, I just . . . ," "I felt in my gut that I should." I have had so many such experiences or insights about what to say or what to do that I had difficulty in choosing anecdotes to set down—but I chose one that relates to my professional life.

One hot July day when I was on vacation, I dropped by my office at Bank Street College. The phone rang. I said to myself, *I'm not picking it up. I'm not even supposed to be here.*

So I let it ring. Then something said to me, *Answer the phone.*

I actually said out loud, "Nah, I'm on vacation." But the phone kept ringing.

I'm not answering that phone. I'm supposed to be at the beach watching the waves.

After three arguments between the phone and the voice in my head, the voice finally, loudly said, *Pick it up* now, *Lorraine.* I did.

The caller said, "I'm calling because I heard you speak recently for the Lilly Foundation in Indianapolis. I have suggested your name as a consultant to go across the United States with three other consultants for the Edna McConnell Clark Foundation. Are you interested?"

"Am I interested?" I had to contain my enthusiasm. I said, "Yes," and I did go. Answering that phone gave me an opportunity to get exposure across America. It made an enormous difference in my career and my life.

Who or what told me to pick up that phone? Who knows? But I'm glad I was listening.

■

Q. Do you ever get messages in the form of "Something tells me . . ." or "I just have a feeling . . . "?

A. Follow your intuition. It can save your career—or your life.

JOKE

1. To make merry, to jest. 2. To excite laughter.

■ Joke around! It loosens the staff up, bonds them together, and re-
leases them to think more freely.

■

The work of the boss is serious and hard. But the boss who can have
fun with his staff and laugh with them—not *at* them—is respected
and appreciated. As Willie Cromer, my mother's father, used to say,
"No fool, no fun!"

When I was working at New York City's Central Board of Education, someone once asked me, "How come you and your team are constantly laughing?"

I answered, "We work twelve-hour days. Try doing that without
having fun. Humor is our way of getting around obstacles and staying
sane while we do it." It must have worked—somehow, in less that a
year, my team and I organized New York's first all-day kindergarten,
planned the new Townsend Harris High School, and set up a partner-
ship between another high school and a four-year college.

Kind laughter is contagious and cleansing. It's unifying, because
what everyone laughs about builds organizational memories that
unite the group: "Remember when we . . . ," "How about the time
when Jo Ann . . . ," "I'll never forget how Steve . . . "

The better I get at what I do, the easier it gets to work lightheartedly
and with laughter.

■

Q. Is there appropriate laughter around your organization? Do you
hear it in meetings? In the halls? In informal get-togethers before
and after work?

A. It's the boss's job to model what kinds of joking are okay and when and where laughter is appropriate. When the time is right and the joking is filled with good humor and positive energy—then laugh! By laughing, you'll free your staff members to laugh with you.

KEEP

1. To preserve, to maintain. 2. To retain in one's possession or power 3. To take care of, to tend.

- Keep the good things that you inherit when you take over an organization. Don't feel the need to change things too quickly or just for the sake of "making your mark."

- Keep doing what works for you—don't change for the sake of change.

■

I have seen very successful organizations fail when the new leader interferes with the inherited organization's way of doing things merely because she wants to put her "stamp" on it. Putting a new "stamp" on an organization may be fine—if the new leader *has* a stamp. But very often the new leader's ego takes over and rather than let the existing success ride, she will undo what's working while having nothing substantial to replace it. This can lead to the destruction of the organization and the departure of its best people.

If you have just taken over a successful organization, don't be afraid to sit still and say to your new staff, "Keep doing what you have been doing." Spend some time watching, listening, and learning. You can enhance the organization's success later on, when you have developed solid ideas for improvement or expansion.

And when you've been following some practice that works for you, don't change it just for the sake of change. I remember some sound advice from one of my assistants, Michael Mirakian, who said to me as I left my high school to go to the Central Board of Education, "Don't change who they hired." I didn't, and it helped me to do good work while there and to remain centered in my belief about who I am and what my future possibilities could be, even when I was let go.

■

Q. Think about your behavior on the job, especially during those times when you feel especially tense, stressed, and challenged. Are you trying to be someone you are not?

A. Remember, you are unique ... and your uniqueness is probably why you were hired in the first place. Of course, you should constantly strive to improve your skills, but don't try to engineer a personality makeover to please others. In the end, you will only betray yourself and weaken the uniqueness that is your greatest gift.

KNOW

1. To perceive directly with the mind or senses. 2. To regard as true beyond doubt. 3. To be capable or skilled in.

- Know the strengths and weaknesses of the people you lead and deploy those qualities appropriately.

- Know your own strengths and weaknesses and use people to complement you.

■

When I became a school principal for the first time, I inherited two first-floor assistant principals whose capabilities and skills I had to get to know in a hurry, since school was to open in a week. I asked my superintendent and his people to give me information about the abilities and strengths of each man. Then I talked to and watched each assistant principal carefully for two or three days.

Based on the information I received, the job descriptions each man wrote for me, and my observations of them, I switched some of their responsibilities. One man seemed to be an ace for detail, paperwork, and getting things done; the other was a people person, the proverbial hail-fellow-well-met. As it turned out, the latter man really was charming, but his lack of interest and skill at handling details was a real liability. Fortunately, the superb detail man (who, as it turned out, also had good people skills) picked up the slack. Before two years elapsed, the people man announced his retirement.

Although I can do paperwork, I am primarily a people person and I don't like paperwork. Recognizing my own interests and strengths enabled me to pull together a team that handled both paper and people efficiently. Achieving this kind of balance helped rejuvenate a moribund high school. I learned at that school that it is the boss's responsibility to build a team with a wide variety of skills.

■

Q. Examine yourself honestly. Which managerial functions do you enjoy the most and handle best? Which ones do you dislike, dread, and mismanage?

A. Rebalance the team around you in order to compensate for one another's weaknesses and blind spots.

Ll

LEAVE

1. To go out of. 2. To go away.

- Leave your leadership position at the top of your game. Then go on to the next dream, which you have fleshed out in your journal or diary and prepared yourself for with courses, contacts, and investments.

- Leave before you are too old or ill to pursue the dreams of your youth—in your youthful fifties, sixties, or seventies.

Leave when you are reluctant to throw your second leg out of the bed. I call this the Second Leg Theory of Leaving. This theory says: When you wake up in the morning to go to work and you put the first leg out of the bed but you want to put that first leg back in the bed and pull the covers up, your clear gut message is that it's time to leave. You have lost the interest and drive necessary to be the great boss. Leave so that you don't destroy yourself and the organization.

Leaving a position of leadership can be difficult even when the work no longer feeds you. For me, leaving is always accompanied by a sense of loss, a loss of the comfort of the known even when the known is not great. Leaving takes courage and a high sense of self and a deep belief that I've been handed an opportunity to create a new life.

A few years ago I successfully headed a subdivision of a very successful company. While there, I felt the security of everything being taken care of. Two years into this work I began to feel antsy, uncomfortable about being totally taken care of, which is really a covert powerlessness.

So I began to plan to be independent, that is, to form my own company (which, by the way, I had been advising women in conferences to do). When I gave notice to the heads of the company for which I worked, they questioned me regarding my preparedness for independence. They were actually quite surprised by all that I had done to be free and independent of them. I now put the second leg out of the bed to work my own business and it feels good.

In one sense, I plan never to stop being a leader. That is, I'll never stop working on my dreams or traveling or thinking or writing or speaking or coaching. However, I will take many leaves, both terminal and temporary: terminal leaves to tackle new challenges in new places, and temporary leaves to do things like:

- go on my second East African safari;

- attend the next international women's conference;

- cruise the Galapagos Islands;

- visit Bora Bora;

- go on an archaeological dig;

- write a play;

- edit my poems;

- somehow be of service to women and young children.

■

Q. What kind of leaves have you taken? What kind do you need to take in the near future?

A. You need to learn to read your internal clock accurately so that you will know when to take your "terminal" leave in order to move on to your new dream. You will notice when you've made the decision how quickly and joyfully the second leg follows the first leg out of the bed.

LINGER

1. To be slow in leaving.

- Linger at work after most people have gone.

- Linger because you can then notice who the lingerers are. They'll notice you, too, and some very productive conversations and ideas can be had at these times. Often these talks can give the leader fresh glimpses into the interests and thinking of staff, and some of the resulting exchanges can be so rich as to contribute significantly to organizational growth.

- Linger with food (coffee, tea, popcorn, and other munchies) for those who drop by to schmooze and bond with the boss.

■

The quiet hours after the phones stop ringing and the customers (students, clients) are gone are often the best times for thinking and doing "donkey/no-brainer" work. These are also great times for bonding with your people. In all of my leadership positions, some of my best moments of learning about my staff and having them get to know me better took place after hours while eating snacks, sandwiches, or meals. Yes, it's even worthwhile to order dinner for everybody and pay for it out of the organizational petty cash drawer or from your own pocket. The conversations that ensue may offer quite big payoffs in terms of organizational growth.

How did we at the Frederick Douglass Academy accomplish the dream of a college preparatory school in Central Harlem? Certainly hard work was a major component of our success, but long hours of planning together were also essential. Over dinner at every faculty meeting, a critical number of staff lingered, ate, laughed, planned, and identified problems and offered solutions.

I fed staff because I come from "foodies," that is, my people love to cook and eat. In my mother's family, to have visitors and not feed them is unthinkable. For me, lingering staff was company. I am hungry at the end of the day because ever since high school, I have had coffee, juice, and vitamins for breakfast and as an administrator I had nothing for lunch—I was too busy going around observing everything. So I'm hungry at the end of the day.

Feeding people is a necessity, and the benefits that accrue to the organization are incalculable.

■

Q. How do you as the boss use your time on the job "after work"?

A. Linger around the workplace and use this schmooze time to deepen your relationships with your staff.

Listen

1. To give heed, to hearken.

- Listen and learn whenever you can.

- Listen and learn wherever you go.

- Listen to advice from a variety of sources.

- Listen to everybody—a few of them may know things you don't!

- Seize opportunities to be quiet and absorb what is vibrating in the air around you, as when you:

  drive

  walk

  play music

  read

  watch children play

  shop

  cook

  do dishes

  do nothing

  wash the car

  garden

  look at the ocean

  watch birds and animals

  ■

Usually the great boss is a quick thinker and sometimes a fast talker because she already knows and has run ahead of the staff in planning and execution. I'm like that, and I confess that I have to consciously bite my tongue or purse my lips to allow myself to hear others. The reason that I have hired smart people is that I want to hear what they think, so I've trained myself to shut up and listen attentively.

I listen not only to people but also for messages from everywhere. I may seem—no, I actually am quite rational in most of my professional dealings. However, when I am not at work, I rely heavily on intuition, the "something tells me" voice that has many times saved my life. This reliance has more than once kept me from harm.

One summer my husband, Hank, and I were on vacation in England's Lake Country, at Lake Windemere, to be precise. I had always wanted to go to this place associated with William Wordsworth. I wanted to recapture his experience of wandering lonely as a cloud. So I arranged with Hank to meet him at the gift shop in an hour. I set off down a lonely, lovely path that had low stone walls on both sides and huge trees with overhanging branches. Lines from "Intimations of Immortality" came to me as I meandered along.

I began, as I moved deeper along the path, to smell urine, human urine. But Wordsworth's lines kept me going. Suddenly, a small brown bird hopped in the path ahead of me and began chirping vigorously. I thought, what a great omen, and I welcomed the bird and kept moving forward. The urine smell grew stronger, but I kept going. The same bird flew in front of me again and chirped twice as hard, its little body contorting into paroxysms. I stopped and watched it, and then it flew over my head behind me and sat in the path in the direction from which I'd come and chirped again. I walked a little further; it flew back over my head and I thought, *What is this crazy bird doing? Is there some message here that I should be listening to?*

The bird sat and chirped wildly. Something said to me, *Go back. Go back fast. Now.* As I retreated, the bird flew away. I turned and nearly ran back to the shop to meet Hank. I never told Hank about the bird until now. But listening to messages from everywhere has been important to me in both my personal and professional lives.

■

Q. When did you last take time out just to listen to what your heart or your intuition was trying to tell you or teach you?

A. Take time to be quiet and pay attention to the voices around you and inside you.

LIVE

1. To pass life in a certain manner as to habits or circumstances. 2. To have an existence rich in experience.

- Live! What is the alternative for a great boss? None. So live!

- Live daily in the present.

- Live well.

- Live wisely.

- Live freely.

- Live foolishly.

- Live frugally.

- Live extravagantly.

- Live quietly.

- Live spiritually.

- Live thoughtfully.

- Live in the future.

- Live uproariously and noisily.

- Live full out, flat out, and real.

■

The great boss needs to know how to live full out, flat out, and real in both parts of his life. For me, I always feel charged up and alive when I drive fast. I love to drive. I guess it's the control, the maneuvering, the competition, whatever.

But on a more serious note, I am wildly alive when I am with my family and my children and their children, who are my extensions in time and place. Being with them can mean doing nothing more spectacular than eating, laughing, talking, walking on the beach, or playing rummy.

In my professional life, I feel fully charged up when I am with colleagues who share my beliefs about the high purpose of education and the function of leadership. I enjoy immensely the loud cross-conversations we have and the exchange of ideas that can happen with other bosses over dinner, in workshops, and in seminars.

The boss must develop the ability to live fully in both her personal and professional life in order to be great and to be balanced.

■

Q. When did you last feel *fully* alive—so deeply in the moment that there *was* no other moment?

A. If you can't remember the last time, reread the list above and think about how you need to change your life.

LOVE

1. To have deep affection and warm feeling for.

- Love the business that you are in.

- Love to perfect your skills.

- Love to expand the meaning of your organization's mission.

- Love to deliver what you promised and more than you promised.

- Love and cherish your past.

- Love your present.

- Love your future.

- Love at least one person immeasurably.

- Love yourself first of all—with deep gratitude to God for the opportunity of being here now, to fulfill what you were sent to do.

■

I love my family and I really love the work that I do. Not only is the work worthy, it is personally fulfilling because doing it requires my head, my soul, my brain, and my personal experiences. I did not want to be an educator, but I knew I wanted to live a life of service to others. My abysmal grades in math made a "counselor" suggest that I teach English, a subject I loved and did well in.

My love for this work increased as my skills increased. I thought of doing something else, but my good results kept me in the work. Once when my superintendent wouldn't give me money to continue a program that was working, I threatened him, saying, "I don't need this job, you know. The telephone company is looking for smart black women." "Okay, okay," he said. I shudder to think what would have become of me if he had taken me up on my threat. Could I have developed a love for that work in the telephone company? Or could I have gone into the seminary, something I had often thought of? The ministry is worthy work, and maybe I could have come to love it as well.

■

Q. What do you love about the work that you do? List three or more things.

A. Examine each item that you listed. Consider whether or not the way you invest your time and energy reflects that love.

Mm

MEDITATE

1. To reflect on; to contemplate. 2. To dwell in thought. 3. To muse, ponder, reflect.

■ **Meditate daily in order to tap into your unconscious wells of wisdom, faith, and power.**

■

When you are constantly going, hurrying and scurrying, you lose composure and the ability to think and lead effectively.

If you don't like the word *meditate,* with its New Age, Eastern-religious connotations, substitute another expression that you are more comfortable with: "Sit quietly," or "Shut off your thinking," or "Stop spinning your mental wheels." Whatever you want to call it, meditation enables the boss to drop her anxiety, to stop going over and over the same problems and coming up with the same solutions.

Meditation for me is important and is crucial to my sanity and my equilibrium as a wife, daughter, mother, boss, and all the other roles I play. I have no special technique, but my routines are as follows:

I choose a quiet place and time, either before going to work or when everyone is asleep or out of the house.

I sit staring at the trees outside my dining room window where birds and squirrels move back and forth.

I breathe deeply.

I read Psalms, especially Psalms 91 and 23, and excerpts from the *Meditations of Marcus Aurelius.*

During meditation I am so susceptible to suggestion that if I read an article about meditation I fall asleep before I finish the article. Interestingly, when I was a very early teen, my father taught me how to relax from my toes straight up my body. Even now, I can never get past my knees before I am totally relaxed or nodding off.

Meditation not only relaxes me but allows my creative mind to come to the fore.

When I want to write or plan, I think of what I want or need to do and then I close my eyes and breathe with my mouth slightly open and fall into a trancelike state. I then naturally wake up to write and plan.

I also have a meditation bowl that I strike. I strike it, then I listen to the reverberations, which stops my mind from racing, which it does a lot.

Meditation sounds vague, but without the ability to calm what Buddhists call the "Monkey Mind," I could not focus on the main thing. When the boss doesn't focus on the main thing, the main thing doesn't get done.

■

Q. Do you take time out to meditate or reflect daily?

A. If not, make room in your life for daily meditation (or quiet time). For most people, meditating before going to work is probably easier and more practical than trying to steal quiet minutes in the middle of the day. The meditation process allows you to find out what you already know in your gut but have overlooked or blocked as too simple and too obvious. Don't skimp on this—quiet time is an essential spiritual nutrient needed in everyone's diet of activities.

MINGLE

1. To combine. 2. To compound. 3. To intermix.

- Mingle with friends and leaders from other businesses or walks of life.

- Mingle with people you don't know at a convention or conference on a subject unfamiliar to you. Help yourself to the free information booklets and giveaways, and take advantage of the opportunity to immerse yourself in a world you've never before encountered.

- Mingle with people from different age groups, ethnic backgrounds, geographic origins, and social circles.

- Mingle and schmooze. You can learn from anybody if you feel and express genuine interest in their work.

■

You need cross-fertilization in order to reenergize yourself and your staff. And you need it in order to tap into new ways of looking at work and life. If you associate only with people who are in the same business as you, you limit your perspectives. You can learn from a plumber, a landscape gardener, a movie director, a fisherman, a Krispy Kreme manager, a carpenter, an endocrinologist, a sanitation worker . . .

I have a neighbor, Ed, who lives down the road from where we built our log cabin. Ed used to raise pheasants for hunters. One day when we walked down to visit him and his wife, Betty, he said to us, "Come on down to the barn to see the pheasants." When we got there, we saw 1,200 pheasants, each one wearing what looked like sunglasses. "What's that those birds are wearing, Ed?" I asked. He responded, "Those are glasses that we put on them to keep them from pecking each other. Wait a minute. You want to see how we do it?" He reached over the wire and grabbed a bird and tucked the bird under his arm. "See," he said. "I catch each bird and then I clamp the glasses on through the two holes in their noses on the sides of their beaks." I said, "You do that to 1,200 of them?" "Yep," he chuckled, proud to teach a New York City high school principal something. "Ed," I asked, "can I have a pair of those glasses?" He ran inside and got a pair for me, which I now carry in my cosmetic case to remind me to ask when I'm confronted with a seemingly impossible task—"is what I'm facing as hard as catching 1,200 pheasants, holding them still, and clamping eyeglasses into their beaks?" I think not.

Associating with Ed and other people who do very different work from me allows me to learn, appreciate, and grow in my own line of work.

■

Q. How many friends do you have who are *not* in the same line of work as you?

A. Make a habit of mingling frequently with people from many walks of life. If you mingle with open eyes and mind, you will learn a thing or two about how to be a better boss. When I watch people in other occupations, I relearn the power of persistence, attention to detail, pride in performance, and sometimes (not often) joy.

Nn

NAME

1. To give a name to, to call. 2. To decide on, to choose.

■ Name your organization and your key projects with special care.

■

Great bosses are careful about the organizational names they choose. Success is sometimes predicated on a name, since the public makes certain assumptions about the organization's mission and its history based on the name.

I recently did some work for a group whose project name was Score High. I inferred from the name that, as earnest as this group's efforts were, they had not scored well in the past and their goal was to score higher the next time around. While the former may be true, why advertise past failures? The external world only needs to know from the name of the project that the goal is maximum success.

The best tactic in naming an organizational project is to let the creatively crazy maniacs come up with a name that denotes the highest level of accomplishment: The Max Scores Program, A-Plus Effort, Project Blue Sky, the Warp Speed Program.

■

Q. What's the name of your organization, or of your newest project or program? What does the name say to people inside and outside of your organization?

A. Let your name suggest the purpose or goal of your organization. Make the name inspiring—a constant reminder of the excellence to which you aspire.

OBSERVE

1. To watch carefully, especially with attention to details or behavior for the purpose of arriving at a judgment.

■ Observe the workings of your organization and its staff every day.

■

My mentor, Mr. Littwin, taught me the importance of observing my staff and the workings of the organization constantly. This requires being present where the work is being done. There's no substitute for *being there*, on the ground, in the thick of the action. As Doreen Land, a successful principal, once said, "If you don't go, you won't know."

I followed Mr. Littwin's advice in my first principalship, and it paid off in large and small ways. First, the level of performance and innovation produced by my staff increased because they knew I would be coming around and they wanted to show off and impress me. This was great for student achievement as well as delightful and flattering for me to see.

Second, the students became accustomed to seeing me anywhere and everywhere at any time, which put the majority on their best behavior. There was even a rumor among the students that I had the power to appear suddenly anywhere in the school. When one brave student asked me, "Is it true, Dr. Monroe, that you can just appear wherever you want in the school?" I replied, with a knowing look and a slight smile, "Yes."

Here's one small example of how being everywhere pays off. One day, an upset parent telephoned me. "Dr. Monroe," she said, "I'm Ms. Greene, and I want to report Mr. Phillips."

"Yes, why?" I asked.

"He assigned the book *Kaffir Boy* and expects my son and the rest of the class to read it in two days. That's impossible."

"Well, Ms. Greene, your son is not telling the truth," I said.

"Really," she shot back, "and just how do you know that?"

"I know," I answered, "because I was in your son's social studies class two weeks ago when Mr. Phillips gave the assignment."

"You were?" Mrs. Greene said weakly. "Oh, then I'd better speak to Josh when he comes home today."

"Yes, I think you should. And maybe you should ask to see his homework assignment book. He does have one, doesn't he?"

"Yes, he does—Thank you, Dr. Monroe—thank you a lot. I'll deal with Josh when he gets home this afternoon."

■

Q. Do you observe some aspect of the workings of your organization daily or, if not daily, at least often enough so that your staff members are not startled or nervous when you drop in?

A. The only way for a great boss to counter complaints is to *know.* The best way to know is to travel around the organization and put your eyeballs or your best assistants' eyeballs on the operation.

OBSESS

1. To influence as by a fixed idea to an unreasonable degree.

- Obsess, but obsess moderately.

- Become a "serial obsessive," always dreaming the next dream.

■

Most successful bosses are obsessives, even if they won't admit it. They are individuals who are driven by an idea or dream that they feel compelled to bull through past all obstacles. This is okay, and may even be essential. Accept your own obsessive quality. But balance your work obsession with other aspects of life—family, friends, travel, relaxation, a spiritual life—so that your psychic, physical, and emotional gears don't get burned out.

One problem most successful obsessives have is an inability to enjoy their victories. As soon as the people around them begin to celebrate, they begin to focus on the next challenge. Again, this is probably a normal and perhaps incurable condition. *Do* go to the party at which the achievement is lauded—it's important to thank your team for their efforts and to let everyone know that you share the joy. Then, reward yourself by going on a well-deserved vacation to a beautiful new environment—and bring along a notebook or journal in which you can start sketching the Next Big Thing about which you will obsess.

■

Q. When was the last time you went home from work without your briefcase or refrained from checking your e-mail and telephone messages as soon as you walked in the door?

A. Be as obsessive about your downtime as you are about your work. You need both!

Participate

1. To take or have a part or share in, as with others.

- Participate in the life of your organization. For example, stop by the employees' cafeteria and lounge regularly. You don't have to sit down if you feel uncomfortable doing so, but stop briefly to greet people, to check informally on projects, and to congratulate the doers.

- Participate by attending staff dinners, luncheons, and games. You don't have to star on these occasions—you just have to be present.

■

The great boss participates to some extent in *all* aspects of the work. And in the nonwork moments, too. I love to laugh, dance, and eat, and best of all I love occasions when I get to do all three. So I'm a big supporter of staff parties, retreats, and informal after-work get-togethers—as well as a major participant in them.

When I was an assistant principal in charge of guidance and pupil personnel services, I worked with Risa Stern, a talented coordinator of student activities. Risa came up with the idea of holding a carnival bazaar fund-raiser on the athletic field behind the school one Saturday.

When Risa asked me to participate, I volunteered to be a fortune-teller. What prompted me I'll never know. I could have sold tickets or made cotton candy, but instead I set up shop in a tent constructed from two king-sized striped sheets under a banner reading "Madame Lorraine."

To my amazement, parents and staff lined up to come into the tent and ask for advice about embarrassingly personal aspects of their lives and relationships. They took Madame Lorraine so seriously that I responded in kind. I found myself speaking truths that came from somewhere I couldn't fathom. Some of my customers warmly thanked me for the wisdom I imparted; others remarked, in tones of astonishment, "How did you know *that* about me?"

Toward the end of the day, I overheard one staff person urging another, "Go on in. Madame Lorraine is really good. Her advice to me was right on the money."

The listener responded, "Nah, I'm not going in there. I've got to work with her on Monday!"

■

Q. Can you name the last three times you took part in nonwork activities with your staff members?

A. Don't be afraid to participate wholeheartedly in the life of your organization. When you do, you're apt to discover new things about yourself and your relationships with your staff.

PENETRATE

1. To recognize the precise nature of. 2. To understand or discern deeply.

- Penetrate behind the presented "facts" or "reality."

- Penetrate and examine the current fad or paradigm to figure out if it's a real benefit to your organization.

■

I was once given the task of teaching ten seventh-grade boys to read. I had never taught anybody to read except my own two children. I'd taught them to read using phonics and sight words that occur often in stories. So I figured I would do the same with the seventh-grade boys.

I bought the familiar green-and-white twenty-six-lettered alphabet chart and put it over the blackboard. We tackled the sounds of the consonants first, then the vowels. I told the boys, "You are not dumb; you just haven't learned to decode. If you were dumb, you could not comprehend what I say to you, which I don't water down. You understand the meaning of words and you can get the main ideas from the stories you read. You can even figure out the characters' motives. You just haven't figured out how to sound out the words that you already know." Little by little, they started reading.

Then one day, the assistant principal called a meeting to tell us about a new way to teach reading. This new technique used an alphabet of forty-two letters. "Soon we will give you books to use in class," the assistant principal told us. I listened and tried very hard not to look skeptical, but I thought, "If the kids can't learn to read with twenty-six letters, how will adding sixteen more letters help matters?"

I got the new books, locked them in the closet, and went back to what I knew worked.

Great bosses always examine closely the efficacy of a hot new concept before using or adapting it. Figure out who benefits by the purchase or use of what is being pushed. Remember what Buckminster Fuller said: "What is going on is never what is really going on."

■

Q. Name the last three Great New Things that have been touted in your field of business or professional activity. Did you opt for any of them? If so, which ones and why?

A. Penetrate the reality behind any person, plan, or new idea. The answer to the question "Who benefits from this?" is often extremely helpful in getting to the underlying truth of many situations.

PERMIT

1. To allow the doing of; to consent. 2. To afford opportunity or possibility.

- Permit the unexpected blessing or good thing to happen.

- Permit others to shine and take the lead even if their actions stretch the rules.

- Permit yourself to be wrong sometimes—and limit your hand-wringing about the error.

■

To believe that you can be a great boss is essential for success. However, to think that you can do great work without permitting others to assist you is foolhardy and egotistical. Allowing others lots of opportunities to think creatively and do innovative work will enhance the success of any organization.

Mr. Waldorf taught a special education class of a dozen students (eleven boys and one girl). Urged by my colleague Dr. Lonnetta Gaines to visit this extraordinary teacher, I went and found, contrary to custom, that his special ed class was not in the basement but in a light, airy fourth-floor classroom. Mr. Waldorf loved little animals, and there were fish, snakes, and iguanas all around the room, swimming, slithering, crawling, and attracting the interest and attention of the students. In the middle of it all was Mr. Waldorf, always on his feet, animated and deeply engaged with everyone.

If you hadn't been told that Mr. Waldorf's students were special education students, you could never have guessed. The first day I visited, the students were using computers to write stories and research information about the creatures in the room. They were also working on a project to breed and sell exotic tropical fish to raise funds for a fishing trip with their teacher.

During my visit, my eye was caught my a huge, very lifelike replica of a giant lizard perched on a windowsill. Marveling at its realism, I approached the model. I was about two feet away when the eye closest to me rotated in its socket. This was no model—it was a real iguana! I let out a little scream, and the whole class laughed with glee.

Later Mr. Waldorf told me that one day the school custodian had reacted to the iguana in much the same way as I had. The next day, the custodian announced, "I ain't cleaning your room no more, Mr. Waldorf. I'll leave you whatever you need—broom, dustpan, plastic bags, whatever. But you won't catch me dead around that monster again!" Mr. Waldorf's kids took on the job of cleaning their own classroom.

On a second visit, I was fascinated by the spectacle of a large boa constrictor, sleeping in a glass tank, while a rat ran frantically back and forth in front of him. Turning to one of Mr. Waldorf's students, I asked, "Why on earth is that rat in there with the snake?"

Without batting an eye, she replied, "Dinner."

Inevitably, someone in the district office heard about Mr. Waldorf's zoo and ordered that it be dismantled. But his principal stood by him. She worked out a set of safeguards to keep the kids and the animals safe and permitted Mr. Waldorf to go on serving his students with his unique and wonderful teaching techniques.

■

Q. What three projects or ideas have you permitted recently that flew in the face of conventional wisdom?

A. The great boss permits her employees to use their talents in any way they can to achieve the mission.

PILOT

1. To lead on a straight and safe course. 2. To guide or direct.

- Pilot with both hands and with your eyes fixed on the harbor—the point toward which you are traveling. Travel with the knowledge that there are copilots, seen and unseen, helping to guide your way.

- Pilot to avoid the shoals and reefs—the rough places that can wreck your chances for success.

- Pilot with knowledge, experience, instinct, and prayer.

■

I've always considered myself the pilot of the organizations I lead. But I always used to say—especially in regard to nonwork activities—"God is my copilot." That is, until one summer in Americus, Georgia, where I worked on a project with Habitat for Humanity, the international home-building organization founded by Millard and Linda Fuller and made famous through the support of former president Jimmy Carter and his wife, Rosalynn.

My work done, I needed a ride to the bus terminal, and two of my fellow volunteers offered me a lift in their car. But when we got in, the darn thing wouldn't start, no matter how often they turned the key in the ignition.

Finally, the two women got out, stood by the hood of the car, and bowed their heads. One of them prayed aloud, "Lord, please help us to get this car started. We have got to get Lorraine to the bus so she won't miss her flight. Thank you, God, for your many blessings. Amen."

I don't think either woman noticed my startled expression. I am a believer in prayer, but it wouldn't have occurred to me to pray for help in starting a car. But when the woman got back in the vehicle, the car started at the first turn of the key.

As we drove toward the bus station, I remarked, "Thank you, ladies. I guess it's true what I always say—that God is my copilot."

"No, Lorraine," one of them quietly corrected me. "God is your pilot."

I thought about this for just a moment—about all the blessings and miracles I've enjoyed in my life, including the successful leadership experiences I've had. Suddenly the truth of her words seemed obvious. "Why, of course!" I replied.

Since then, I've been careful to remember and acknowledge who the real pilot is, in both my professional and personal life.

■

Q. In your role as Chief Pilot, who or what helps you to avoid the shoals, reefs, and rapids?

A. Steer your vessel with full awareness that there are copilots, seen and unseen, who are continually active in your work and your life.

PLAN

1. To devise. 2. To arrange the parts of a program. 3. To project the realization or achievement of.

- Plan for the most important aspects of your dream.

- Plan several ways to achieve your dream.

■

It's important to have a great Plan A in which you believe and to which you are committed. But to avoid being caught flat-footed in front of your staff in the event that Plan A doesn't work (hey, it happens), you need Plan B and even Plan C.

Generally speaking, Plan B should simply embody an alternative path toward achieving the same mission as Plan A. The goal and the focus remain the same; only such specifics as timetables, key players, and the sequence of events change. You should be able to shift from Plan A to Plan B if necessary with speed and assurance.

If you have to move to Plan C, however, it may be time to rethink the mission. Sometimes radical changes or circumstances you don't control force a fundamental shift in the organization's direction. This is not always a bad thing. One of the biggest mistakes a boss can make is to insist on pursuing a plan that has stopped working.

■

Q. Have you planned out your mission? Can you write down your Plan A in one sentence? Do you have a Plan B? Write it now, too.

A. Sometimes Destiny frustrates your Plan A and Plan B because she has something exciting and new in mind for you. Listen to her!

Prepare

1. To make ready beforehand for some purpose, use, or activity. 2. To put in a proper state of mind.

- Prepare yourself for a future you can't predict.

■

After my mentor, Mr. Littwin, said, "You would make a good principal," I knew I had to go to school to get state certification. Something told me to go right away. As with everything in my life, I am either in some strange mode of comfortable stasis or I am running headlong into a future whose outcome I cannot even imagine.

I'd certainly never imagined myself as a school leader. I was a successful English teacher, and I loved the work of teaching—especially English. I had done it for almost two decades. But Mr. Littwin's words stirred something in me that said, *Find a graduate school and get busy getting ready.* And I became driven to get prepared.

In one semester and one summer school session, I earned the eighteen credits necessary for state certification as a school principal. When I returned to work that September, Mr. Littwin called me into his office and said, "Lorraine, Mr. Gonzalez, the second assistant principal, has taken an emergency leave. You can have the position if you have your certification."

The moment he finished, I said breathlessly, "I received it in the mail last week." Thus began my leadership march.

■

Q. What are you doing today to prepare yourself for tomorrow's challenge?

A. You may not know what the next challenge will be—but if you are growing and learning today, you are getting prepared for it. You'll probably find your path and the next challenge intersecting at an interesting place just around the next corner or over the next hilltop—tomorrow.

PRESENT

1. To put before. 2. To offer to view.

- Present the truth of any organizational problem judiciously to your staff both in private gatherings and in large groups.

- Present your congratulations to your staff for work well done in immediate love-notes, in public meetings, and in staff bulletins or newsletters.

- Present yourself to your staff as a facilitator—that is, as someone who gets things done, makes things happen, and makes progress easier.

■

A great boss has a variety of ways to present himself and the mission to his staff. One of my favorite ways was to use a weekly staff bulletin. I made sure that the bulletin always opened with a wise saying or pithy quotation designed to inspire and focus the staff's attention on a specific aspect of our work. Then I used the rest of the bulletin to:

- highlight group accomplishments;

- congratulate individuals on a job well done;

- reiterate policies and practices that were being forgotten or overlooked;

- remind staff members about what I'd be looking for in my rounds that week;

- present ideas for future development and exploration;

- invite volunteers for special projects;

- focus the staff on a particular theme for the week.

In short, the bulletin was designed to be a written reminder of what I believed and expected and of our organizational mission—something that could speak for me and represent me in times and in places where I couldn't be present.

■

Q. How are you using the opportunities you have to communicate with your staff?

A. Your organization probably offers many opportunities for you to present yourself: a newsletter, a regular staff meeting, a weekly "memo from the boss," a bulletin board, a regular companywide e-mail. Take advantage of these opportunities and make sure that you send a message that is clear, consistent, upbeat, and focused.

PRESERVE

1. To keep safe from injury, harm, or destruction.

■ Preserve a sanctuary or meditation refuge in your organization for quiet thinking (*not* the staff lounge) for yourself. It could be a corner in your office with a favorite chair, special paper, a favorite pen, a replica of a favorite painting, plants or collected stones, feathers, shells—any items that help you to regroup, decompress, and put things, people, and events in proper perspective.

■

After a year as a boss, I came to realize that not every problem is arterial bleeding. I understood that if I wanted to stay in the work and remain sane and productive, I could not be 100 percent available 100 percent of the time.

In my first job as principal, one of my office walls had two windows onto the hallway through which my staff members could look as they walked past. Sometimes I would be sitting occupied with work and I could hear them say, "I see her; she's in there."

My dutiful secretary would protest, "She's busy," but they would interrupt anyway. "I know, I know," they would reply, "but this will only take a minute." *Nothing* takes only a minute, and they knew they were lying when they said that, but I always buckled and gracefully allowed the intrusion.

In self-defense, I created a sanctuary in the only place they could not get to me—my little private bathroom down the hall. I placed a chair in there, a Bible, and pens and paper. It was my own Winnie-the-Pooh thinking corner. I planned many a great project in there.

As fate would have it, in my second school, my conference room had no windows. Lucky me!

■

Q. How can the great boss who wants to inspire, communicate, observe, teach, lead, discipline, listen, and challenge . . . do all those things while preserving her sanity?

A. Create a sacred space or refuge, away from your office, where only one person—your secretary, chief assistant, or second in command—can find you.

QUEST

1. To search. 2. To ask for. 3. To go on a quest.

- Make time for yourself and others to search for personal meaning in the work.

- Plan a time during staff retreats for individuals to go on solo "Vision Quests."

■

The quest for bliss and balance is of extreme importance for all leaders. However, this quest has particular urgency for many women leaders. Indeed, as I was writing this entry, it was startling for me to be brought face-to-face with the reality that I function as boss, daughter, sister, wife, mother, grandmother, aunt, colleague, and friend—often all in the same day. So my quest, like that of most other thoughtful leaders both male and female, is to seek the following:

- to be good in order to do good

- to nourish my body and my soul in order to nourish others

- to understand who I am and why I am here in this position in this place at this time

- to serve something higher than self

- to be worthy of the charge that has been given me

On my daily walkabouts, I always carried a journal or notebook in which to jot questions that occurred to me as well as the answers I derived from the work of my star performers. Every week or two I would review these notes and update and improve my plans and strategies based on what they taught me. The result was an ongoing quest to improve the life and health of the organization.

■

Q. Can you list at least three things that you are searching for in your work or through your work?

A. The responses to the question above should elicit honest, thoughtful answers that enable you as leader to be more mindful of the serious aspects of service and leadership.

Rr

Recall

1. To remember what has been learned or experienced. 2. To bring back to mind.

■ Recall how you were led as a child and as a young professional. Draw from these recollections the lessons you need as to how (and how *not*) to lead others today.

■

When I was a young teenager, I attended Julia Ward Howe Junior High School in Central Harlem. It was headed by a great principal, Anna E. Lawson. In later years, I remembered not only how well the school was run, but also how smart I became in that school. So when I got to be boss, I tried to emulate Ms. Lawson's style and replicate her vision.

Under my mentor, Mr. Littwin, I learned how to monitor instruction and how to make a vision pervasive in an institution. The list below indicates the characteristics that Ms. Lawson and Mr. Littwin shared despite their differences in gender, age, and ethnicity. Both leaders:

- had a vision of what a great institution could be, which was palpable upon entering the front door;

- held their staffs accountable for maintaining high expectations in order to get good results;

- had a commanding presence that could be intimidating when they chose to display it;

- accepted no excuses;

- took no prisoners;

- were omnipresent;

- were able to attract, hire, train, and retain committed staff members;

- could strike fear in the hearts of incompetents, who either changed their ways or left;

- had the respect of productive staff members;

- encouraged and mentored others to become leaders—even at the price of losing them.

Is that an impressive list of qualities? Indeed it is. Just recalling what made those two leaders great has been enough to give me a lifetime's worth of leadership lessons to emulate, study, and practice.

■

Q. Look at the list of leadership qualities above. Which of these qualities do you possess? Which ones do you need to develop?

A. Recall the great bosses you've worked under or heard about. Think about how you can emulate their best qualities while maintaining your central core—what makes you you.

REDUCE

1. To bring down as in extent, amount, or degree; to diminish. 2. To lower in range or grade; to decrease.

■ Reduce useless clutter in your work environment.

■ Reduce the amount of time you listen to bitching and moaning from your staff. Limit gripe sessions to three minutes.

■ Reduce off-task preoccupations, such as gossiping, taking every telephone call, checking voice mail and e-mail constantly, and giving ear to the drop-by visitor.

■

Success in reducing physical and mental clutter gives you more time to focus on the things you are always saying you would do if only you had more time.

Anytime you allow some staff or individuals who drop by to sit down you lose a half hour of precious time and reduce your productivity. There are chronic "this will only take a minute" people. I identified who they were and usually I would see them coming, stop them at the door before they could get a seat, and say, "Let me walk you to your next place."

Of course, you have to know your people in order to separate those who just want to be in the presence of the boss from those who actually have an idea or suggestion to move the mission.

I once broke my rule of allowing a person to come in and sit down who had never spoken in a meeting or even spoken to me more than briefly. He apparently heard me in a staff meeting when I announced that I was open to innovative projects that would help our students. As soon as he sat, he said, "I have an idea." He had a great idea. It involved having students do serious community service in the local bank, hospital, and school. Many students benefited from this experience. The school was on the six o'clock news because the program he instituted was so successful.

I made an exception to my rule. Remember I said reduce, not eliminate, drop-by visitors because you never know who the bearer of the Next Big Idea will be.

■

Q. Estimate how much time you spend dealing with interruptions. What things or persons are distracting you from your real work?

A. Looking at your list, write three ways you will reduce or eliminate these distractions in order to increase your effectiveness as boss.

Reflect

1. To consider mentally. 2. To turn thoughts back upon something.

- Reflect on how blessed you are. You are a leader; that means you have been given the chance to make a dream come true by what you plan and what you make happen.

- Reflect daily on what you've done. Assess whether or not you could have done it better. Make a better plan for tomorrow based on your reflections.

■

Not only is a great leader a reflective practitioner—she also teaches others to reflect.

One year I bought inexpensive notebooks for all the members of my staff. At the beginning of one of our monthly faculty conferences, I handed them out, saying, "These are reflection journals. Please take five minutes right now to jot down some thoughts about your successes, your failures, the things you've been trying, and your ideas and dreams about your work and your own future."

I had no idea how the teachers would respond. But perhaps because they saw my assistants and me journaling, they fell to writing without a question. It warmed my heart to see these experienced teachers bent over their journals, pens wagging, like kids taking an exam. When five minutes had passed, I announced, "Time's up," and I collected the journals. We went on with our regular agenda, and I kept the journals in our conference room. Five minutes of journaling became a regular part of each meeting thereafter.

I never read any of the journals. At the end of the year, many of the teachers took their journals. Much later, one of them told me, "You know that journal you made us keep? I still have mine, and I still write in it. It has helped me think through some really tough problems. Just thought you'd like to know."

Q. Does your staff have time built into their schedules to permit them to reflect on their work?

A. Adults need to learn to carve time out of their busy lives to reflect on what is happening to them. We often have experiences whose significance we miss. Journaling is a wonderful way of uncovering the inner meaning of our lives and our work. Sometimes the thoughts we capture in writing may end up being of great importance to us and our organization.

RELEASE

1. To set free from restraint or confinement. 2. To relieve from something that confines, burdens, or oppresses.

- Release the powers of your Talented Tenth. Turn them into a think-tank team of crazy dreamers from across the organization's departments. Meet once a month for an open, no-holds-barred session around a concern, idea, upcoming project, or a "Why can't we . . . " or "What if . . . "

■

The great boss doesn't wait for 100 percent of her staff to understand the dream. There are talented staff members hiding even in what external people consider a moribund organization, and these individuals must be released from the confines of the bureaucratic organization chart to become the heart of your change effort.

W.E.B. DuBois spoke of the Talented Tenth—a small group cultivated and developed that will ultimately lift the people, or, in this case, lift the organization. No boss moves an organization forward without finding, supporting, and rewarding this Talented Tenth. They've been waiting and longing for a great boss to come, release them, and allow them to fly. When this happens, some others in the 90 percent will catch fire from the activity, productivity, and excitement of the top 10 percent, and they will begin to move, because most people want the boss's approval and notice for doing the right things.

■

Q. Can you list the Talented Tenth in your organization?

A. Identify your Talented Tenth, meet with them, listen to their ideas, support them, and let them run.

REST

1. To cease from action. 2. To pause. 3. To be at peace.

- Rest and come back rejuvenated. Built-in breaks are essential to the success of a leader: 100-percent accessibility = 100-percent disaster for the organization and for the leader (or for any person, for that matter).

- Rest with no regrets. Ban all work and work-talk from leisure time with your family and friends.

- Rest for real. This will save your brain, your organization, and your life. Every two weeks, take a rest day—all day Saturday or all day Sunday. Rest can be gardening, golfing, daydreaming, or driving—any actions different from your ordinary daily work.

■

When I was working at 110 Livingston Street, the headquarters of New York's Central Board of Education, it was a rare day when I didn't have a dozen appointments back to back. I didn't eat lunch. Instead, I drank tea and snacked on raisins and nuts. I got in at 7:30 A.M. and often left twelve hours later.

I was actually unaware of the hours I put in daily. One day when my secretary gave me the appointment schedule for the day, I saw it, as if for the first time, for what it was—punishing. The next day, it occurred to me to insert a fictitious person for a twenty-minute slot, so I wrote on my schedule the name "Max Goldman." While I sat in my office with the door closed, supposedly waiting for Mr. Goldman to show up, I drank a cup of herb tea and read a few excerpts from the great Roman philosopher Marcus Aurelius. At the end of twenty minutes, my secretary announced the next appointment. I felt refreshed and ready.

I continued this practice, eventually developing a system of rotating fictitious names (after my secretary threatened to call Mr. Goldman to berate him for continually missing his appointments).

Q. Do you plan so that there are rest periods in your day, week, month, year?

A. Make sure you get enough rest to keep you happy, healthy, and working at your utmost potential.

RETHINK

1. To reevaluate. 2. To reconsider. 3. To recheck.

- Rethink your first ideas before making them public.

- Rethink how your organization is pursuing its original mission.

- Rethink who's doing what in your organization.

- Rethink your personal leadership style.

■

Rethink and change any of these if there is need to do so; some shifting in any of the above can reinvigorate the organization.

For the great boss, rethinking the first idea is fun and is as productive as the thinking that produced the first plan. The main reason is that you are probably smarter in the rethinking than you were in the first thinking.

Rethinking what and who is good for the organization is often not easy for the great boss to do because it means letting people go who are retarding the forward movement of the big idea. I inherited a man in a position of some authority, a head of a department. He was in place when I came on board. Being new, I did not want to make too many major changes at once, but in a very short time I realized that he was not the right person for the position. He did not control his staff. He ran an Old Boys' department in which there was poor performance, excessive absences, and latenesses that were covered up. To make matters worse, he did not follow up on my decisions and edicts. I spoke to him. I then moved to written requests and demands. He retired within a year.

In another instance, I had to rethink whether or not to retain a person who was in a position of authority. He did not have the respect of his staff, nor did he have the energy necessary to monitor his workers.

It was particularly hard to let him go because I knew him from a former place. It was difficult to put friendship aside, but I had to for the good of the organization. When I finally called him in to notify him that I was removing him from his responsibilities, he seemed neither surprised nor upset. Actually, he was relieved. He too left at the end of the year and went on to excel elsewhere in an entirely different position for which he was better suited.

Having led schools twice and educational programs several times, rethinking is second nature for me. I simply use all that I learned from my earlier attempts and augment it with my newest thoughts and experiences. Letting people go is never easy, but it is a crucial part of the invaluable exercise of rethinking for a leader.

■

Q. When is the last time you rethought the essential purpose of your organization and the roles that key staff play in accomplishing the purpose?

A. To rethink and replan is a pathway to rejuvenating your organization and maintaining excellence.

RETREAT

1. To withdraw; to draw or lead back.

- Retreat periodically from the hubbub of daily work to make long-range plans that will energize and excite everyone on your team.

■

During my years running high schools, I used the technique of an annual retreat as a vital punctuation mark in the year. Just before Labor Day, we brought the old and new staff together for a day and a half away from school, where we were removed from the distractions of the familiar workplace. I always chose a lovely resort not so far from the city as to be daunting but far enough away to discourage driving home at the end of the day, since some of the most productive conversations and bonding took place after the leisurely dinner and the crazy dancing of the first evening.

The retreat workday lasted from 8:30 A.M. to 4:00 P.M., after which people could use the gym, pool, tennis courts, or bowling alley. But we did work hard, reviewing and assessing the past year, setting the theme for the new year, and making specific plans for increased academic achievement, increased activity by our sports teams, and increased community involvement in the arts, charity, social programs, and so on. We blocked out the entire year from September to June in terms of exam preparation, special events, and established traditions.

It was quite satisfying and comforting for old and new staff members alike to leave the retreat with specific marching orders and plans in their hands. We all felt prepared for the coming school year and upbeat about the success and possibilities that come from concrete planning.

■

Q. How long has it been since the members of your leadership team have had a chance to retreat from day-to-day activity and look at the big picture together?

A. Find a time and a place to take a deep breath and think about your organization's past, present, and future (as well as to have some crazy, creative, productive fun). The result will be increased energy, excitement, and enthusiasm that will help carry you forward for months to come.

SACRIFICE

1. To surrender something desirable on behalf of a higher object or a claim deemed more pressing.

- Sacrifice time, money, and personnel when necessary to get the work done well and quickly—but never sacrifice your core principles and beliefs.

■

For great bosses, the most pressing claim is the creation of a successful organization, i.e., one that is meeting its goals.

All decisions and actions in the organization must lead to the accomplishment of the goal. Thus, great bosses make every sacrifice in pursuit of this end—doing whatever it takes. Full devotion to the cause is absolutely necessary. What is the alternative? There is none.

Schools, businesses, most enterprises, and most human beings fail when they have not figured out what they stand for, that is, what their core principles are. These are generally best expressed in a simple mission statement. Once the mission is understood, then obstacles of time and money must not be allowed to impede the forward movement toward that goal. When the goal is paramount, the amount of time spent on the clock and off the clock is not even discussed. Either money is gotten or the need for money is gotten around.

Once, at the Frederick Douglass Academy, we wanted to start a tap-dancing class. My uncle Harold Cromer is one of the old tappers—Stumpy in the tap team of Stump and Stumpy. He offered to give our students tap-dancing lessons, but we had no tap shoes and no money for them.

One afternoon, several of us sat around thinking about what to do. The next day, our shop teacher appeared with a sample tap that he had made from hammering flat the bowl of a teaspoon. He was all ready to get to work producing enough taps for the whole class, using pieces of discarded flatware!

Ultimately, that wasn't necessary—we got money for our tap-dancing program through the Committee for the Twenty-first Century. But I kept that battered teaspoon in my desk for years as a symbol of the can-do spirit of people who signed on because they believed in the mission and who were creatively crazy about the principles of the enterprise.

■

Q. Can you name three sacrifices you've made recently to further the work of your organization?

A. Look for opportunities to give up things you value in exchange for things of greater importance for you and for the mission of your organization.

SANCTIFY

1. To set apart as dear to. 2. To dedicate, to set aside a part in honor of. 3. To make inviolate, that is, not to be profaned.

- Sanctify your work by:

  caring

  making sure it is worthy

  making sure that it helps both your staff and your clients

  making sure it does not exploit workers or the environment

- Sanctify your work by inspiring people to do their best in order to make a difference in the world.

- Sanctify your work by creating win-win situations. When the clients are winning, we win. When the clients profit, we profit.

■

To speak of spirituality or holiness in the workplace seems strange to some people. But every organization has an unspoken sense of purpose that is palpable in the way people deal with each other, with the clients, and with the outside world. The sanctity of any organization's work comes from its sense of purpose as expressed through the heart, head, and mouth of the boss. Thus, sanctifying your work and your workplace begins with dedicating *yourself* as a vessel for whatever spirit you serve.

■

Q. In what ways are you keeping the core mission of your organization sacred and untouchable?

A. Make certain that everyone in your organization understands what is sacred, what's not, and why. Don't let trivial matters related to bureaucracy, turf, or egos be transformed into "sacred cows" that people are afraid to question. But be certain that the core values are understood and respected as the heart of your organization.

Select

1. To take by preference from among others; to pick out; to choose.
2. To choose from among several; to pick out the best.

- Select the best staff members you can—the real doers—and meet with them early so that they understand the ethos of your work and the way work is done in your organization.

- Select sterling internal mentors/buddies for new hires. Support and reward buddies who show new hires the ropes. If time permits, let new hires watch the mentors and others in order to see various aspects of the organization's work.

■

Select new hires very carefully. After introducing new hires to the entire staff, allow two weeks before you, the boss, monitor their work. However, during this period, the veteran staff should be monitoring the new hires' work regularly. Retaining new hires should depend on the early assessments of the boss and the mentors. Retention of a hiring mistake can cause the boss to lose youth, beauty, and sleep.

I once made a bad hire because school was about to open and I needed the position filled immediately. So I hired in haste and out of desperation, which, like marrying under the same conditions, leads to regret. I hired a bad person who lacked both people and work skills. The telephone recommendation from her former boss indicated neither deficiency. The new hire's unreasonableness, which was evidenced early on, was a cover-up for her lack of ability. We learned to work around and behind her, which was totally unfair to her coworkers.

Another bad hire was a man who came to fill a vacancy as a per diem substitute in a hard-to-fill area. His résumé was incredible. He had been everything except a fire chief. I soon found out that he couldn't teach to save his life, but he developed such a "swell" relationship with the kids (by not giving homework or having lesson plans) that he was quite popular. He soon became popular also with two other malcontents who were borderline unsatisfactory teachers.

When I complained to my superintendent, he said to me, "Lorraine, never believe anybody with a résumé like that. Didn't you ask yourself why a man with a background like that would want to be a substitute teacher in junior high school if he had done and had been all of those things?"

I said, "You're right, but I needed a math teacher desperately." I let Mr. Wonderful go in mid-December—still with a hole in my staff, but smarter about the next selection.

Having been burned twice, I made a new policy: Any prospective staff person had to demonstrate his or her teaching ability before hiring. How had this simple selection technique eluded me?

■

Q. Have you ever—great boss that you are—selected a dud?

A. If you have hired a dud—and if that dud is still on staff—let the person go, humanely but promptly. Then think about how you can make a smarter hiring decision next time.

Shed

1. To cast off; to rid oneself of.

- Shed your inhibitions—your "I don't know if I can" and "I don't know if I should."

- Shed the fear that sometimes makes you doubt yourself to the extent that you think, *Maybe they hired the wrong person,* or *Maybe I'm not as good as they think I am,* or *Maybe I'm not as good as my last triumph.*

- Shed the loser mentality right away and get new skills to augment the great ones that got you to be boss in the first place.

■

How do I shed my fears and inhibitions? I have many ways. Here are a few I like.

I learn how others have accomplished what I want to accomplish. I'm a voracious reader of books in the areas of self-help, psychology, health, fitness, and spiritual growth. I watch TV shows that feature writers, chefs, explorers, archeologists—anyone who has dared greatly and accomplished great things. If they could do it, so can I.

I take courses unrelated to my present work. The value of these courses varies and is impossible to predict beforehand. I took "Counseling the Culturally Different Woman," and I loved it. I took "How to Make Slides and Other Audio-Visual Teaching Aids," and I bombed—I still stick to good old white boards and markers. I took "Mid-Life Crisis Counseling," and I found it terrific—in fact, I used it on myself. I took "Learn to Speak Italian in Three Hours"—and I didn't.

In each case, I learned a lot about myself. I also learned more about how to work with others. Above all, I shed some of my inhibitions by plunging at full speed into uncharted territory, relying (as always) on prayer, meditation, and my sense of high adventure.

■

Q. Can you list three inhibitions you need to shed?

A. Pick one inhibition and take a stab at shedding it. Write down what happened and how you felt after this first attempt. When you have successfully shed one inhibition, work on shedding a second . . .

Shelter

1. To cover or protect.

■ Shelter your organization against the constant winds of change by maintaining your focus on the core mission.

■

Every field—education, business, government, medicine, law—has its fads, its crazes, its trends, which change constantly. While one of these fads is on the rise, it can exert enormous pressure on your organization to change in response to the fad. The only remedy is to hold fast to the core mission, which should not shift according to every Next New Thing.

A good leader shelters her staff from internal and external pressures and influences. For example, in education, there are frequent mandates and suggestions about how to do the work, driven by political and economic conditions as well as by academic fancies. Successful schools, like successful businesses and other organizations, always examine the "new ideas" with an open but skeptical mind. The new ideas generally are not really new but are the same-old, same-old—reconfigured with different languages, format, grids and graphs, and new names, all of which sells books, texts, and tapes. The great boss takes the parts that are valuable for improving his particular work and ignores the rest.

Thus, the wildly successful organizations are led by surprisingly old-fashioned individuals—what I call Radical Traditionalists. As a Radical Traditionalist, I see my job as sheltering my organization from crazy pendulum swings. This takes both sound judgment and guts— but you have both; otherwise, why would you be the boss?

■

Q. Which old ways of doing things are at the core of your organization and need to be held on to, no matter what?

A. Be a Radical Traditionalist. Try bold new ways of staying focused on the powerful old goals of excellence and productivity.

Simplify

1. To show an easier or shorter process for doing.

- Simplify operations with explicit instructions.

- Simplify the mission so that everyone can state it in a phrase or simple declarative sentence.

■

I have found that staff will almost never tell you that they don't understand what you said they should do. Don't wait for them to speak up—spell out what must be done with utter clarity, whether your staff expresses confusion or not.

If the mission is stated in a paragraph, no one on your staff will be able to state it. And if your staff can't state it, they can't make it happen.

Here are some examples of simple mission statements:

"Our mission is to make the best can openers in the United States."

"Our mission is to send all of our students to college."

"Our mission is to create beautiful, affordable housing for low-income people."

■

Q. Can you list existing operations, methods, and systems in your organization that need to be simplified in order for you to move forward more quickly and effectively? Can you write your organization's mission in one simple statement?

A. A simplified mission statement is the leader's chief tool for making better decisions. The mission statement enables the boss to test every act or proposal against the organization's stated purpose.

STRETCH

1. To reach out, to extend. 2. To amplify, enlarge, or expand.

- Stretch yourself and your organization beyond its comfort zone.

■

I have seen bosses lose greatness mainly by not stretching themselves beyond their own habitual behavior—familiar ways of managing that used to work but that no longer apply. This usually happens through laziness, misplaced egotism, or fear. It takes real mental exertion to unrut yourself from the comfort zone of "We used to . . . " and "We always . . . ." Fear of what change can bring has hampered the growth of many bosses and their enterprises.

Of course, I'm not immune from this problem. When my children were young, I did not stretch my career path. I liked classroom teaching and never thought to examine whether my comfort zone was inhibiting my growth. I spent more than fifteen years in the classroom happily—joyously—teaching English.

It was only after my husband got a job teaching in college and the children were enrolled in after-school sports that I sat back and reviewed my situation. After years of contentment, I suddenly felt ill at ease. In a moment of epiphany, I unrutted myself into graduate school and within a few years into school administration.

Later, as a boss, I learned to constantly watch my organization's comfort zone, looking for opportunities to stretch beyond it. I transposed to my workplaces my personal bias for always having some project, program, or idea on the back burner to begin working on as soon as the present project was completed. I was amazed to find that my staff loved being part of an organization where we held on to the core mission at the same time that we were always stretching to develop new and creative ways of doing the work.

■

Q. Are the people in your organization contented with the status quo?
   Are you?

A. Perhaps you're not being stretched enough by the goals you've set
   and the methods you're using. List what you could be doing more
   of. List the exciting new targets your organization can aim for.

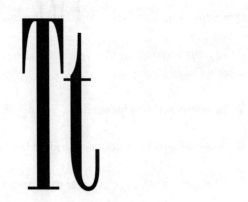

TAKE

1. To get possession of; capture; seize. 2. To carry, convey, or lead to another place.

- Take responsibility for results.

- Take risks that keep you alert and on the cutting edge.

- Take complete charge in order to move projects faster.

- Take advantage of an opportunity when it comes along, even if it is not the opportunity you've been praying for.

■

In every leadership position I have held, I have taken hold of the work and thereby taken the organization to another level.

For my first principalship, I was assigned to a large high school as an interim/acting principal. In my mind, "interim/acting" is a bogus category; it means that you do the work of the position but get paid at the level of the position you just left. So I never took this designation seriously.

At the end of my first year, a team of performance review inspectors came to write a report for my superintendent and Chancellor Macchiarola outlining the progress I'd made. After the inspectors toured the school and read through the material I'd prepared, one of them turned to me and said, "How did you do all of this? You are only an *interim* principal."

I looked at him squarely and said in a slightly flippant tone, "I've never been an interim anything in my life. When Chancellor Macchiarola congratulated me in August, he said, 'Ms. Monroe, go be principal.' I took him at his word, and I did just that."

■

Q. What three things in your organization do you need to take control of—*now?*

A. You can't be tentative about leading. Either you lead, or someone else in the organization will. So when the opportunity arises, take the reins—or know that someone else will take them. If that happens, forget about being the boss—let alone a great boss!

THINK

1. To form or have in the mind. 2. To exercise the powers of judgment, conception, or inference.

■ Think backward—start with the outcome, goal, or result clearly in mind, then figure out a way to achieve that goal.

■

So many of our wasted efforts come from our failure to think through and communicate clearly the objective *before* we begin. For example, I remember attending a workshop that failed in its purpose because the directions for getting to the desired outcome were extremely complicated. The workshop participants and facilitators spent half of the workshop time interpreting the convoluted instructions. Instead, the mission should have been clearly and simply stated: "At the end of this workshop, you will leave with the following body of knowledge."

This could have happened if the planners had started by thinking backward—that is, by beginning with the end or goal in mind:

• What do we want the participants to know?

• What simple steps must they take to accomplish this?

And most important, before promulgating the directions, the workshop leaders should have walked through the steps themselves to catch the glitches and to simplify the instructions. It is remarkably easy for bosses to understand what they want done, because what they want done is their own idea. But if the boss fails to check whether the directions and the plan are clear even to those with no prior knowledge, confusion and disaster are inevitable.

■

Q. In your various plans, or dreams, have you run ahead mentally and on paper to think through specific strategies, personnel, and schedules to be used in achieving your goal?

A. Desired outcomes occur when leaders run ahead mentally (and sometimes physically) in order to anticipate and eliminate anything that might get in the way of success. Think through your dreams and then put the plans in place.

TRANSCEND

1. To rise above or beyond. 2. To surpass or outstrip.

- Transcend all personal pettiness and institutional obstacles to your goals.

- Transcend because of your high sense of the rightness of your goals.

- Transcend difficulties because when you are moving in the right direction, helpers in many guises will unexpectedly appear in your life. They will permit you to vault over those difficulties you could never conquer alone.

■

I have worked hard on many projects when I had no idea how I would get them done. I could see the obstacles rising around me; I could hear the doubts and objections from everyone who knew me; the way over the difficulties remained invisible. But eventually, the solution always turned up—somehow. It might come in the form of a telephone call from someone I'd never met or an appointment with a person who had come to see me for an entirely different reason. However it happened, I'd somehow be handed the very thing I needed to accomplish my goal.

One time, I'd been looking for some way to develop a community of scholars to help energize a group of up-and-coming schools in minority neighborhoods. Out of the blue, a man who had heard about our work at the School Leadership Academy came to see me. "You don't know me," he apologized, "but I'm looking for a way to introduce more young minority students to a scholars' program I'm heading. I don't suppose you'd be interested in working with me on this?"

All I could do was laugh. We'd soon outlined a miniproposal for the program that later turned into a full-blown proposal for a major funding source.

■

Q. Can you name two instances when you transcended obstacles that you thought would be major stumbling blocks?

A. Dream big, even when the difficulties seem bigger than the opportunity—someone or something will usually come along to help you transcend the obstacles and make your dream come true. To paraphrase the words of the old spiritual: You make a way out of no way.

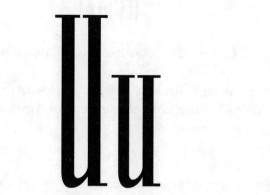

Uplift

1. To elevate; to raise aloft. 2. To better in condition.

■ The job of the leader is to uplift her people—not just as members of and contributors to the organization, but as individuals of infinite worth in their own right.

■

Every great boss knows that the success of the organization depends upon producing tangible outcomes. The nature of these outcomes depends on the organization. In a for-profit business, they may include greater sales, increased profits, better product quality, larger market share, or increased stock value. In a not-for-profit organization, they may include more clients served, increased efficiency, and an expanded mission.

Objectives like these are important. But organizations that survive and thrive even in rocky times do something more than meet tangible objectives. They also attract and retain star talent because the staff is uplifted by the spirit of the leader.

Everything the leader does can contribute to this sense of uplift. It grows out of the speeches the leader makes, the informal interactions between the leader and the staff, the clarity and boldness of the strategic vision set forth by the leader, and above all the visible activities of the leader and the example these activities set. To be most effective, everything the leader does should focus simultaneously on two objectives, the growth and development of the organization and the growth and development of the staff as individuals.

However, to be able to uplift an organization in this way, a leader must first be uplifted himself by the organization's purpose, and, second, his motives for wanting to be boss must be 99-percent pure.

■

Q. Can you support both objectives—the growth and development of the organization and the growth and development of your staff as individuals—in everything you do?

A. If you actively support the development of your organization and your staff, your staff will be uplifted beyond petty concerns (raises, promotions, office politics) and inspired to accomplish the larger win-win mission of the organization.

VALUE

1. To estimate the worth of. 2. To set great store by. 3. To hold in high esteem, to prize; to appreciate.

- Value the hard effort and good work done by your staff. Let them know!

- Value the precious time you have on earth to be a great boss; your time is quite short in the grand scheme of things. Avoid evil and destructive things, people, and behavior.

- Value the good results that come from being with, laughing with, talking with your staff.

- Value the joy you get from doing worthy work.

■

Great bosses show that they value the good work of their staff in simple and complex ways. Of course, staff members like to be given immediate verbal praise for a job well done. And they appreciate more formal recognition—in written notes, public awards, acclaim in meetings and staff bulletins, and so on.

Somewhat to my surprise, I also learned that staff members value a boss who recognizes the difference between real producers and "shuckers and jivers"—that is, those who talk a good game but do very little.

In my first principalship, I spent all of September observing every teacher for three to five minutes each, so as to get a fix on who was doing what and at what level of proficiency. I spotted one veteran teacher who obviously was doing no real teaching. I began to observe him frequently, looking for a way to train him to teach. But I soon discovered that he was incapable of learning. (This, despite twenty years of satisfactory ratings from my predecessors.) With my encourage-

ment, he transferred to another school at the end of the year, and retired from the school system one year after that.

When the rest of the staff saw that I was able to recognize the differences among different levels of teachers, they began to give me consistently what I wanted—an honest day's work of bell-to-bell teaching
that steadily increased student achievement.

■

Q. What do you value in your staff members? How do they *know* what
you value?

A. Make sure your staff knows the value you place on their work. Setting an honest, accurate value of the work done by your staff—both
the great work and the not-so-great work—will help generate serious commitment from everyone on your team.

Ww

WAIT

1. To hold back expectantly.

- When faced with an important decision, wait! Avoid making decisions on the run.

■

I often had wily staff members waylay me when I was on the run. They wanted to suggest one of their pet projects in moments when I could not think clearly. They would intercept me on my way in or out of the building, in the hallway or the elevator, in the ladies room, or in the parking lot.

If you are not wary, you may agree to something in haste that you will regret at leisure. I learned to say, "Make an appointment with my secretary so that we can talk about your idea at some length. Better yet, give me a one-pager on it."

If they are in earnest, you'll hear from them again. Notice, I did *not* say, "That sounds like a great idea, make an appointment . . . " because they will hear nothing after the words, "That sounds like a great idea." They will start moving on their idea, which *may* be great but then again may require some fast footwork to undo.

■

Q. When rushed or pushed, have you ever made a snap decision that you lived to regret?

A. Learn to take a deep breath and count to ten when feeling harassed into making a quick decision. Wait and then ask for the details and insist on taking the time required to examine them. Your staff members will soon learn to expect a thoughtful decision-making process from you—not a hasty one.

WRITE

1. To set down for others to read. 2. To communicate a message using words.

- Write love notes.

- Write slam notes.

- Write brief memos.

- Write thorough Memos of Understanding to follow up on conferences with individuals whom you are attempting to help, correct, train, and/or castigate.

- Write thank-you notes.

- Write a weekly or monthly bulletin or newsletter.

- Write your own boss brief notes to keep her abreast of things.

■

Put it in writing! Writing clarifies your message, reduces misinterpretation, and holds staff members accountable—especially if the memo or announcement is distributed at a meeting that you know they attended where the content was discussed and explained.

Recently I was asked to counsel a group of leaders whose staffs were not following the leaders' mandates. When I asked the leaders about how they informed staff about what they expected, each one began by saying, "Well, I tell them . . . "

I hastened to say to them that they have to document their expectations in writing; otherwise, they cannot hold staff accountable for results. I further explained that their written expectations must always include due dates and succinct information about who does what, when, where, how, and why. Staff members should sign a receipt that they received the written expectations, and lastly, these expectations should be posted in prominent common meeting places.

As detailed as the above may seem, paper is proof against both negative employees who are reluctant to do anything the boss wants and reluctant employees who are too embarrassed to admit in public that they did not understand what the boss wanted.

Oral instructions are only effective with self-motivated employees, and even self-motivated employees can use the written expectations as a reminder or checklist.

■

Q. How often have you communicated with your staff in writing during the past month?

A. Use written messages whenever the content is complex, important, or of lasting value. Some people never quite believe that you mean what you say until they see it in black-and-white print. So put it in writing, and eliminate all doubt.

Xx

X–RAY

1. To penetrate through various thicknesses of solids by rapidly moving cathode rays.

■ X-ray your organization and its people. Examine your organization's hidden inner workings so that you can accurately appraise your staff members and the degree of talent, commitment, and energy they bring to the work.

■

Great bosses have the capacity to penetrate—that is, to see through—some very thick solids. This includes penetrating the kind of convincing but ultimately meaningless B.S. that some staff members become artists at spreading. You know the kind—I'm referring to people who, when you spot them doing little or nothing (or only *bad* things), offer excuses like:

"You caught me at a bad time."

"The work was going great until you walked in."

"As soon as you left, the work got going great."

"I could really produce for this organization if only I had better [equipment, support, students, staff, time, space, supervision, opportunities . . . you name it]."

I can generally spot these B.S. artists from a long way off. Occasionally, however, my X-ray vision breaks down. Whenever I've hired in haste because I desperately needed a body to fill a position or because I was facing a systemwide scarcity of talent, I've made the mistake of turning off or ignoring my X-ray vision. I always came to regret the results.

■

Q. Have you developed the X-ray vision a great boss needs to see through the excuses that nonperformers try to hide behind?

A. Practice using your X-ray eyes, and don't ever be lulled into shutting them when hiring, evaluating, and training your staff.

Yield

1. To give, restore, or produce. 2. To give place to, as to something superior.

■ Yield control, authority, and influence to those who truly deserve it—people who are as devoted to the mission as you are and who possess some knowledge or skill you don't have.

■

No leader can be brilliant in every aspect of the organization's work. Therefore, you must be able to recognize in others the talents that you lack. It takes great ego strength to do this and to yield to others when necessary. It forces you to seek out, recognize, make room for, and honor others who do what you dislike doing or what you cannot do well.

I recognize in myself an ability to conceive and plan new projects; this is my delight. But niggling, exact details are less interesting to me. Fortunately, I've been blessed to attract extremely intelligent assistants who not only think well and fast but are detail oriented and able to point out lapses or holes in the plan that must be fixed so that the project goes off without a hitch. These people have saved me from disaster more often than I can say.

(Interestingly, I'm often able to recognize the holes in *other* people's plans—just not in my own. I suppose this is ego again. Or perhaps it's just because, once I've dreamed up a project, I'm already thinking about the Next Big Thing.)

■

Q. How well do you know yourself and your staff, your strengths and your weaknesses? Have you analyzed which elements of your power you can yield without losing authority and control?

A. Do the hard work of learning your abilities and your limitations, and when necessary be strong enough to yield to others who bring to the table the talents you lack.

Zz

Zigzag

1. To take a series of short, sharp turns in a course or path.

- Don't be afraid when things don't go the way you expect them to go. Look for the hidden blessings in the zigs and the zags.

■

The path of the organization is rarely straight. Neither is your path in life. The great boss expects the sharp turns and remains calm while navigating them.

When I was a novice English teacher in East Harlem, the principal of our high school, Leonard F. Littwin, was offered the opportunity to open a brand-new high school in the Bronx, to be called Adlai Stevenson High School. When the staff got wind of the news, a frenzy of gossip whipped around the building. Everyone wondered who would be chosen to go with Mr. Littwin to the new school and who would be left behind.

There was a group of about half a dozen teachers who took particular pleasure in stoking the rumor mill. They were all convinced that they were going to Stevenson, and they talked about this constantly among themselves and with anyone else who'd listen. Others on the staff—including me—fell silent in the face of this group's self-confidence and their glee at the prospect of leaving the rest of us behind.

For some reason, several in the group of self-anointed Chosen Ones decided that I ought to join them in the exodus. They urged me to apply for a transfer to Stevenson. "You know I'm a new teacher," I protested. "I don't have the years to qualify for a transfer." They poohpoohed my doubts and continually badgered me to apply. I remember glancing out the door of my room in the middle of a class and spotting a couple of these "Goers" walking slowly past, mouthing the word "Apply!" and making thumbs-up gestures in my direction. I was flattered by their attention, but I knew the rules, and I had no intention of applying for a transfer.

Finally, on the deadline date for transfer applications, two of the Goers cornered me in the school office. "Listen, Monroe," one of them insisted, "This is your last chance. Write a note to the boss—tell him you want to go to Stevenson with us."

"Okay, okay," I replied. To appease them, I tore a sheet of paper from my plan book and scribbled on it, "Dear Mr. Littwin, Take me along," and signed it.

A few weeks later, I was stunned to learn that I'd been chosen to go to Stevenson—and not a single one of the supposedly Chosen Ones had been picked. I certainly had no idea how the selections were made (and I'm sure the Chosen Ones found it even more baffling than I did).

So my scribbled note to Mr. Littwin ended up taking me on an amazing career zigzag. I left behind a troubled school and moved to a brand-new school where I improved my teaching skills, got the chance to serve as a dean of discipline, and later became an assistant principal. In time, thanks in large part to Mr. Littwin's powerful mentorship and tutelage, I ultimately led two high schools and later moved on to the Central Board of Education of New York City as deputy chancellor for curriculum.

But here's the strangest part of the story. While serving as Mr. Littwin's assistant principal, I made a startling discovery. Cleaning out my predecessor's desk, I came across the old list of who was to go to the new school and who was to be left behind. My name was on the list of the stay-behinds!

What had happened? How and why did my name zig from one list and zag onto the other? What angel had stepped in and thereby changed my professional life forever? I'll never know. But the story shows how big a role Destiny plays in all of our lives—for better or for worse.

Sometimes the better and the worse are almost inextricably intertwined. That's what happened years later, when I was summarily dismissed from my job at the Central Board of Ed.

I still remember the sense of shock, dismay, hurt, anger, and humiliation I felt when I read the curt letter of dismissal. We've all told friends who face the same situation, "Don't take it personally," but that advice is almost impossible to follow. Our work is deeply bound up with our lives, our dreams, our aspirations, and our sense of identity. When that work is snatched away, how can we *not* take it personally?

After regaining my composure, I began to ask myself, "Now what?" Answering that question took weeks. I spent many days alone in my apartment after my husband, Hank, went off to work. I played gospel records over and over again. (I practically wore a hole in one record: "God Is Not Through with Me Yet.") I put on loud dance music and cavorted around the living room until I was drenched in funky sweat. I cooked and cleaned.

Yes, I did some serious work, too. I worked on completing my doctoral dissertation (while listening obsessively to still more music, this time Keith Jarrett's album *The Köhn Concert*). I taught a graduate course in the evenings at the Bank Street College of Education.

Most important, I took the time to think about what this zigzag meant and to explore the new pathways that this latest twist might lead to. Eventually, I found a whole new aspect of my work that I would probably never have uncovered if I'd remained at the Board of Ed— namely, working as a consultant to schools and school districts.

By tossing me out of my niche, the system had forced me to discover a new way of working, one that has proven to be more exciting and liberating than I could ever have imagined.

■

Q. What zigzags has your life's path taken? What lessons have you learned from those sudden twists of fate?

A. The zigzags we encounter on our life's journey can be frustrating and scary. We dream that life will follow a smooth, straight path. But zigzags come, and when they do come, don't panic. Learn to go with the flow. Your next zigzag may turn out to be a wonderful gift in disguise.

EPILOGUE

Monroe's Twelve Pieces of Parting Advice*

1. Step out on faith and create your own future.

2. Believe in the power of transformation and astonish yourself.

3. Accept the challenge and forge ahead.

4. Transcend rage.

5. Use creative solitude.

6. Know that there are always options and alternatives.

7. Prepare and be ready for unexpected miracles.

8. Take well-calculated risks.

9. Put one foot in front of the other; keep moving.

10. Find the gift that stands in the midst of pain and change.

11. Remain focused on the main thing.

12. Rock steady.

* Turn to these whenever the need arises.

POSTSCRIPT

Last year while writing a note to a friend, I made two spelling errors whose double entendres—double meanings—I pass on to you, dear Boss, as a postscript. Make of them what you will.

∎

Pray attention.
God bliss you.

ACTION PLAN WORKSHEET

GOAL STRATEGIES	RESOURCES NEEDED	DATES	EVIDENCE	RATIONALE
What do I want to achieve?	What actions will I take to make my goal happen?	Who or what will help me achieve each strategy?	When will each strategy be completed?	What will I see or have that shows I have completed each strategy?
RATIONALE: What existing conditions made me choose this goal?				

Appendix

The Action Plan Worksheet

The success of any project, program, or idea rests solidly on good planning. The Action Plan Worksheet is the tool we use at the Lorraine Monroe Leadership Institute when assisting organizations, departments, and individuals to plan for success.

Here's how to use it:

1. Fill out the worksheet months before the plan is to be put into operation.

2. In the first column, describe the goal you want to achieve. Beneath that, briefly describe the rationale for choosing that goal. (You'd be surprised to learn how often the rationale for a goal is somehow forgotten long before the goal is achieved!)

3. In the second column, list the specific actions you and your team will take to accomplish your goal. Number these in sequence.

4. In the third column, write the name or position of the person(s) responsible for each action.

5. In the fourth column, write a definite date for the completion of each action.

6. In the fifth column, write the tangible evidence that you the leader (or someone you designate) will observe to prove that each action has been completed—a progress report or final report, a signed-off checklist, a finished letter or memo, a contract draft, a sample product, whatever.

7. Write a new Action Plan Worksheet for the next important project.

You may want to rough out an Action Plan Worksheet for yourself before meeting with your planning group or trusted inner circle. Once the worksheet has been put into final form, distribute copies to everyone in a leadership role on the project, and refer to it at every check-in meeting. Soon everyone on the team will be using the worksheet as a guide, reminder, and schedule, insuring that the whole organization is (literally) on the same page in regard to this project.

ACKNOWLEDGMENTS

I owe deep thanks and appreciation to the people listed below without whose help, encouragement, and examples I could never have done this:

Peter Osnos

Karl Weber

Kate Darnton

Dr. Lonnetta Gaines

Dr. Henry Monroe

Anna E. Lawson

Leonard F. Littwin

Reverend James H. Robinson

PUBLICAFFAIRS is a publishing house founded in 1997. It is a tribute to the standards, values, and flair of three persons who have served as mentors to countless reporters, writers, editors, and book people of all kinds, including me.

I. F. STONE, proprietor of *I. F. Stone's Weekly,* combined a commitment to the First Amendment with entrepreneurial zeal and reporting skill and became one of the great independent journalists in American history. At the age of eighty, Izzy published *The Trial of Socrates,* which was a national bestseller. He wrote the book after he taught himself ancient Greek.

BENJAMIN C. BRADLEE was for nearly thirty years the charismatic editorial leader of *The Washington Post*. It was Ben who gave the *Post* the range and courage to pursue such historic issues as Watergate. He supported his reporters with a tenacity that made them fearless, and it is no accident that so many became authors of influential, best-selling books.

ROBERT L. BERNSTEIN, the chief executive of Random House for more than a quarter century, guided one of the nation's premier publishing houses. Bob was personally responsible for many books of political dissent and argument that challenged tyranny around the globe. He is also the founder and was the longtime chair of Human Rights Watch, one of the most respected human rights organizations in the world.

. . .

For fifty years, the banner of Public Affairs Press was carried by its owner Morris B. Schnapper, who published Gandhi, Nasser, Toynbee, Truman, and about 1,500 other authors. In 1983 Schnapper was described by *The Washington Post* as "a redoubtable gadfly." His legacy will endure in the books to come.

Peter Osnos, *Publisher*